A HISTORY OF ENGLAND

General Editors

CHRISTOPHER BROOKE, M.A., F.R.Hist.S.
Professor of Mediaeval History
University of Liverpool

and

DENIS MACK SMITH, M.A.
Fellow and Tutor, Peterhouse, Cambridge

Vol. 8

Volumes in the series

Modern Britain

1885-1955

HENRY PELLING

Thomas Nelson and Sons Ltd   Edinburgh

THOMAS NELSON AND SONS LTD
Parkside Works Edinburgh 9
36 Park Street London W1
512 Flinders Street Melbourne C1

302–304 Barclays Bank Building
Commissioner and Kruis Streets
Johannesburg

THOMAS NELSON AND SONS (CANADA) LTD
91–93 Wellington Street West   Toronto 1

THOMAS NELSON AND SONS
19 East 47th Street New York 17

SOCIÉTÉ FRANÇAISE D'ÉDITIONS NELSON
97 rue Monge Paris 5

———

First published 1960

© Henry Pelling 1960

General Editors' Preface

KNOWLEDGE and understanding of English history change and develop so rapidly that a new series needs little apology. The present series was planned in the conviction that a fresh survey of English history was needed, and that the time was ripe for it. It will cover the whole span from Caesar's first invasion in 55 B.C. to 1955, and be completed in eight volumes. The precise scope and scale of each book will inevitably vary according to the special circumstances of its period ; but each will combine a clear narrative with an analysis of many aspects of history —social, economic, religious, cultural and so forth—such as is essential in any approach to English history today.

The special aim of this series is to provide serious and yet challenging books, not buried under a mountain of detail. Each volume is intended to provide a picture and an appreciation of its age, as well as a lucid outline, written by an expert who is keen to make available and alive the findings of modern research. They are intended to be reasonably short—long enough that the reader may feel he has really been shown the ingredients of a period, not so long that he loses appetite for anything further. The series is intended to be a stimulus to wider reading rather than a substitute for it ; and yet to comprise a set of volumes, each, within its limits, complete in itself. Our hope is to provide an introduction to English history which is lively and illuminating, and which makes it at once exciting and more intelligible.

C. N. L. B.

D. M. S.

Author's Preface

THE reader will find that the chapters of this book have a
uniform arrangement. Britain's external relations, both economic and political, were of such fundamental importance in
this period of the nation's history that I have placed them first.
Accordingly, the opening section of each chapter deals with
foreign and Imperial or Commonwealth affairs, and also
includes a narrative of military operations in wartime. A
second section of each chapter deals with domestic politics and
legislation, and a third and final section endeavours to describe
the major trends of social change.

Two of my colleagues at The Queen's College, Oxford,
Mr B. F. McGuinness and Mr Geoffrey Marshall, have
very kindly read this work in typescript, and by their sug-
gestions have helped to improve it in a number of ways.
The editors of the series, Professor Christopher Brooke and
Mr Denis Mack Smith, have performed a similar service.

H. M. P.

Contents

List of Plates

*Acknowledgment is made to the Radio Times Hulton Picture Library
for permission to use the photographs reproduced in this book. The
graph on page 197 is reproduced by courtesy of the Fabian Society.*

1 Britain in 1885

IN 1885 Queen Victoria had been on the throne for forty-eight years : she was to live for another sixteen years more. This volume thus begins three-quarters of the way through the 'Victorian Age', and some apology might seem to be needed for breaking into the conventional unity of the reign. But by this time the influence of the Crown was no longer so great as to dictate the character of an age : and in reality the year 1885 forms as good a starting-point as any other for the study of modern Britain. In the economic sphere it was notable for that questioning of accepted assumptions of natural progress and prosperity which led to the Royal Commission on Industry and Trade, 1885–6 ; politically it saw the virtual achievement of manhood suffrage by the Reform Act of 1884 and the Redistribution Act of 1885. From the interaction of these two themes, so emphatically stated at the start of the period that we are to examine—the theme of Britain's economic vicissitudes and that of her entry into a period of political democracy—we may trace out many of the major developments of the succeeding seventy years of history.

★

By the early 1880's Britain—if not the United Kingdom as a whole, which then included all Ireland—had already acquired many of the characteristics by which we know her in the mid-twentieth century. Her rapid industrial growth in the preceding century had made her a predominantly urban nation, supported by a large foreign trade. She was dependent, as never before, upon imports of raw materials and food, and she paid for these by the export of her manufactures, or by other goods and services. Her population in

1

1881 was thirty million ; fifty years later it was to be half as large again, but fifty years earlier it had been only sixteen million. The cities had been growing at a proportionately much faster rate : London had doubled its size in a quarter of a century ; and the urban centres of industry, such as Manchester, Birmingham, Sheffield, and Leeds, had increased at an even greater speed. By 1881, although the population of the rural areas had remained more or less constant, the proportion of Britain's inhabitants living in urban areas was over two-thirds.

It is not difficult to explain these rapid changes. The Industrial Revolution which had already been transforming Britain a century earlier had acquired momentum. It is true that the expansion of the cotton industry, judged by the size of its labour force, was substantially over by 1851 : in that year it employed 527,000 workers, a total not much exceeded in later years. But the impetus given to the heavy industries—coal, iron and steel, and engineering—was more lasting. The coal industry employed 216,000 in 1851, but the figure had gone up to 382,000 in 1881, and was still quickly rising. In iron and steel and in engineering the increases were even more rapid, owing to the stimulus of new inventions and processes. These industries produced an increasing flood of producers' goods, that is to say, the machines that would in their turn increase industrial production, whether at home or elsewhere. They also made the railway rolling stock and locomotives, and the steamships, which helped to speed up communications throughout the world and so to quicken world trade. In the early 1880's almost a half of the value of all British exports was in textiles (three-quarters of this in cotton) ; almost another quarter was in coal, iron and steel, or engineering.

Yet in spite of the sensational progress of the preceding century, economists and City men alike were no longer happy about the future prospects of British trade. Investors could not now make the large profits of fifteen or twenty years earlier ; in some export fields there was stagnation ; and in the 1870's, and again in the mid-eighties, there were prolonged periods of ' bad trade ', with consequent idle plant and a high level of industrial unemployment. As a result some observers were beginning to speak of a ' Great Depression ', which they dated from about 1873.

It was in agriculture that the onset of depression was most marked. This was perhaps only to be expected, for the system of free trade naturally exposed the farmers to heavy competition from abroad in a world eager to pay for British industrial exports by means of agricultural produce. Yet transport difficulties had long kept off the full force of this competition ; and rents and land values in Britain continued to rise until the end of the 1870's. By this time the existence of an agricultural depression was acknowledged by the appointment of a Royal Commission on Agriculture in 1881 : yet its conclusion was that the distress was due to a series of poor harvests occasioned by abnormally bad weather. In the early 1880's, however, it became more obvious that the growth of American agriculture and the improvements in shipping facilities were having their effect. British wheat prices dropped sharply, farmers fell into arrears with their rents, and large tracts of arable land went out of cultivation. Between 1879 and 1887 the permanent pasture of Britain increased by a million acres. Nor was this all : for in the same period the technique of sending frozen and chilled meat from Australia and New Zealand was introduced, and so the British meat market was the scene of heavy competition. The wages of British agricultural labourers fell, and the real depopulation of the countryside—as distinct from the migration of excess population due to natural increase—now began in earnest. In Scotland many of the landlords, despairing of receiving adequate rents from their crofter tenants, evicted them and turned the land into estates for grouse shooting ; in Ireland a new crisis arose between tenant and landlord, and because the latter was so often an absentee in Britain this gave fresh impetus to the Irish nationalist movement.

If this had been all in the way of economic distress, it would have been bad enough. But further complications were caused by the fact that foreign countries were now building up their own industries, usually behind high tariff protection, and consequently many of the best British export markets were being lost. The most important industrial competitors of Britain were the United States and Germany,

whose progress in the 1870's and 1880's was exceedingly
rapid.   The increase of coal output and of the production of
iron and steel in these countries was far in excess of that of
Britain, although Britain still remained the largest producer
in both spheres.   In new industries, moreover, such as chemicals and the electrical trades, Germany and the United States
were establishing an early lead.   When the slump of the
mid-eighties took place a Royal Commission was set up to
inquire into ' the Depression in Trade and Industry ', and it
had no difficulty in diagnosing the evil : ' We are beginning,'
it reported, ' to feel the effect of foreign competition in quarters where our trade formerly enjoyed a practical monopoly.'

What was the remedy ?   The Commission had no clear
answer.   Farmers and manufacturers for the home market
tended to favour the abandonment of free trade and the
return to some system of protection.   A ' Fair Trade League '
to press for this had already been founded in 1881.   Exporters,
however, felt that this would lead to retaliation by other
countries, which would reduce their prospects even more.
They had no real alternative policy, except to hope for better
times and to search for fresh markets in the farthest corners
of the world—which, fortunately, were always becoming more
accessible as improvements in transport took place.   If Europe
and the United States would not buy British, then it was
necessary to appeal to Asia and to Africa and to the British
colonies.

At this time the proportion of British trade that was
absorbed by the British possessions was not particularly large :
it amounted to about one-third of total exports.   The manufacturers of the United Kingdom had in the previous generation made as easy an entry into independent countries as into
the dependencies of the Crown ;   and economic historians
speak of Britain's ' informal empire ' of commerce as an area
different from and much more extensive than the ' formal
empire ' which owed allegiance to the Queen.   In the middle
of the nineteenth century, indeed, the colonies appeared to
be of no real value to the home country.   Many of them had
to be secured by garrisons of British troops, but there were
no obvious compensating advantages for the heavy expenditure that this involved.   In this period even Disraeli had
(2,274)

spoken of ' these wretched colonies' as ' a millstone round our necks '.

In the 1870's, however, this attitude began to change. It was partly a matter of national psychology, the desire to show that, in a world of rapidly growing empires like those of the United States and Germany, there was none to equal the global vastness of British possessions. Sir John Seeley's book *The Expansion of England* (1883) put the case for emigration to the colonies as a way of building up British power— although at the time the majority of British emigrants were still going to the United States. To some extent a new acquisitive policy developed as a result of the attitude of the colonists themselves : the Australians, for instance, insisted on the British occupation of New Guinea in 1883. But beyond all this there was the feeling that British rule was the best way of safeguarding commercial advantages : not that ' trade followed the flag ', but that the flag could and should maintain trade built up under conditions equitable to all comers. Although Gladstone and the Liberals were more reluctant than the Conservatives under Disraeli to see extensions of imperial control, from the 1870's onwards governments of both political complexions adopted much more positive policies than they had hitherto done. Thus it was Gladstone's Government which in 1882 took the important step of occupying Egypt in order to set right that country's chaotic finances and administration.

*

Meanwhile the choice of members of the House of Commons, the final arbiter of British policy, had been placed in the hands of the people. Up until 1867 the franchise had been a limited one, but the Second Reform Act of that year had given the vote to the bulk of the working class in the borough constituencies. The county franchise remained restricted, and much remained to be done to equalise the size of constituencies. But sooner or later, it was clear, the final steps of creating a popular franchise would be taken. The Third Reform Act of 1884 and the Redistribution Act of 1885, both of them passed during Gladstone's second administration, effected the anticipated changes ; the working classes in the counties were now given the vote, and the country was divided up into constituencies of roughly equal numerical size. Some anomalies remained, such as the university seats, and there was still a certain bias in favour of the more sparsely populated areas. But by and large the radical principle of ' equal electoral districts ' had been brought into practice ; and with the stringent limitation of electoral expenses by the Corrupt Practices Act of 1883, it seemed reasonable to assume that in the choice between parliamentary candidates the popular will would in future prevail.

But what was the popular will ? The more widely extended the franchise, the more sectional and localised were the political opinions that it expressed. With the advent of democracy the deeply rooted differences between Englishman and Welshman, or Lancashireman and Yorkshireman, came to the fore as they had never done previously. National resentments and religious prejudices of a traditional, inherited character bulked larger than any demand for social reform. During the 1870's the Liberal Party became more and more the agent of the nonconformist interest, which attacked the Church of England, demanded strict temperance legislation, and urged the establishment of a secular state system of education (without public support for the voluntary schools of the Church). On the other side, the Conservatives defended the Church of England, sought to protect the interests both of the voluntary schools and of the public house, and sometimes demanded an increase in expenditure on the army and navy. It is easy to trace a correlation between Liberal voting and those parts of the country where nonconformity was strong ; in fact, the old industrial areas of the eighteenth century, where the inflexible parish system of the Church of England had been unable to cope with the demands of a sudden increase of population. The whole of Wales was also Liberal, for national as well as religious reasons : the fight to disestablish the Church there was a fight against an alien domination. Conservatism, on the other hand, was strong in the south and east of England, in parts of Scotland (where national feeling was less affected by a feeling of inferiority), and also in Lancashire and Cheshire, apparently in part as a reaction of the indigenous population against the immigrant

Irish who numbered about a quarter of a million in these
two counties.

All these differences found their representation in two
political parties : for it was now true of Britain—though not
of Ireland—that, as Guardsman Willis pointed out in the
Gilbert and Sullivan opera *Iolanthe* (1882) :

> Every boy and every gal
> That's born into the world alive
> Is either a little Liberal
> Or else a little Conservative !

But the multiplicity of interests in each party was never far
beneath the surface. Each party, in reality, was a coalition,
brought together for parliamentary purposes under one outstanding leader, and always threatening to fall apart when no
such single leader was available. One element in each party
was a section of the old aristocracy, which derived its interest
in politics and its attitude largely from family tradition. But
also there were new elements rising to power as agents of the
new electorate. In the Liberal Party, Joseph Chamberlain,
an industrialist who had been a highly successful mayor of
Birmingham, had in 1877 organised a body called the
National Liberal Federation, which was a grouping of the
new type of constituency associations. This body, largely
urban, largely nonconformist, disputed with the aristocratic
Whigs for the control of the party, with Gladstone as a
somewhat reluctant arbiter. In the Conservative Party there
was a corresponding extra-parliamentary organisation, the
National Union of Conservative and Constitutional Associations, formed in 1867, and at first much less popular in
composition ; but the young Lord Randolph Churchill, sens-
ing the needs of the new electorate, demanded an alteration
of the party structure in order to give the Union more power
and a more representative character. He also founded the
' Primrose League ', a propaganda body which rapidly
attained some social importance, if not political power, by
admitting women to its membership. This activity by
Churchill was not regarded with much enthusiasm by the
older Conservative leadership under Lord Salisbury.

Churchill had realised, as Disraeli had done before him,

that large sections of the working class were prepared to associate themselves with the Conservative Party, provided that they were given the opportunity. It is true that the articulate leaders of the manual workers—the trade-union officials, who now represented a total membership of between a half and three-quarters of a million—tended to be Liberals, because they were mostly the products of a nonconformist environment ; indeed, the first Members of Parliament from this class, two in the 1874 Parliament and three in that of 1880, had joined the Liberal Party in the House. But they could not speak for the working class as a whole, and it was obvious that in rural England, as well as in London and Lancashire, there was plenty of labour support for the Conservatives on the various issues that divided them from their political opponents. The Trades Union Congress itself recognised this in its instructions to its Parliamentary Committee, whose duty it was to lobby governments of any political complexion in the interests of the unions ; and one of the Liberal-Labour Members of Parliament said of Disraeli's Government of the 1870's that ' the Conservative Party have done more for the working classes in five years than the Liberals have in fifty '. He was referring to the Government's work in legalising peaceful picketing (Conspiracy and Protection of Property Act, 1875), in passing an important Housing Act, and in reducing the factory working week to 57 hours instead of 60.

Early in the 1880's, however, the issue that increasingly dominated British politics was that of Ireland. Agricultural decline, the reasons for which we have already mentioned, resulted in the eviction of tenants, and evictions in turn led to outrages. Parnell, the Irish Nationalist leader, urged that everyone who abetted evictions should be treated ' as if he were a leper of old '. The first person to receive this treatment was one Captain Boycott, and this gave rise to the new word ' boycotting '. An Irish Land League to defend the tenants sprang into existence : at the end of 1880 its leaders were prosecuted for conspiracy, but after a jury disagreement they were acquitted. In 1881 the Liberal Government was forced to pass a Coercion Act to try to restore order, but it made little difference ; the disorders culminated in the murder of the Liberal Chief Secretary, Lord Frederick Cavendish, in

Phoenix Park, Dublin, in 1882. Gladstone at the time was
trying to come to terms with the Irish parliamentary leaders :
he introduced a generous Land Act, passed in 1881, the
operation of which led to a gradual restoration of order.
Meanwhile Parnell, with a disciplined parliamentary party
of over sixty members and with a carefully mobilised Irish
vote in the British constituencies (consisting of the Irish
immigrants, of whom there were about 560,000 in England
and Wales alone), angled for bids of alliance from the British
parties, seeking always to secure the prize of Home Rule.
He negotiated first with the Liberals, through Chamberlain,
and then with the Conservatives, through Churchill. At the
1885 elections he decided to switch the Irish vote to the
Conservatives, probably calculating that they would then be
dependent on Irish support to form a government. His own
party, gaining from the new electoral changes, rose to a total
of 86 ; but as it turned out, this number was exactly equal
to the majority of Liberals over Conservatives in the new
House. The only hope of a stable government lay in the
collaboration of Liberals and Irish.

★

Social divisions in late-Victorian Britain were much more
marked than today, and especially the great gulf which
separated the ' respectable ' people from the manual labourers.
This gulf did not have anything quite to correspond to it in
politics, for politics were as yet ' respectable ' and had not
been adapted to a condition of universal suffrage. But there
was a great contrast in dress, manners, and way of life
between the better-off and the poor. To a considerable
extent this was because social life centred on the home—and a
home without the levelling influences of radio or television.
For the better-off people, woman's place was in the home—
not so much for the sake of performing domestic chores, since
domestic service was cheap and abundant, as for supervising
the conduct of a large household and entertaining visitors.
Families were large in those days : over a quarter of the total
population were children under the age of ten. Only the
women of the working class took paid employment—for

instance in the Lancashire and Yorkshire textile industries, or more generally throughout the country in domestic service. This resulted in a considerable difference of dress : ' ladies ' wore impractical, fashionable clothes, tight corsets to achieve the ' wasp waist ' effect, and bustles to accentuate it ; working-class women were more sensibly if less attractively attired. Even among men there were marked social differences of costume : the business man wore his conventional ' topper ' and frock coat, with trousers trailing behind the heel ; workmen had not yet given up corduroy and fustian.

There were, however, signs of change. Many of the distinctions had been due to the tendency of the newly rich to ape the airs of the aristocracy. But as time went on the growing middle class began to establish a less formal and less expensive code of its own. Things which the aristocracy could do at home, the new suburban families had to arrange in association. Just as the local political association was the middle-class counterpart of the ' influence ' of the country house, so the ' public ' (really ' private ') school took the place of the private tutor, and organised games formed a substitute for the week-end house party. At the beginning of the 1880's the bicycle was just coming in and was welcomed as a useful alternative to the horse. By the 1870's the movement for the foundation of new universities to rival aristocratic Oxford and Cambridge was developing ; and Oxford and Cambridge themselves, if still largely the preserve of the wealthy, had at least been opened to nonconformists. Even girls' education, which lagged behind that of boys, was being organised : the Girls' Public Day School Trust had lately been established, and colleges for women were being founded in the old university towns.

Between the middle class and the working class, however, substantial differences remained, even though the better-off workers, and more especially their wives, eagerly sought to emulate their social superiors. The main barrier was that of inferior education. It was only in 1870 that the state education system had been introduced, and only in 1891 that it became both universal and free up to the age of twelve : universal, that is to say, for the poor, because the children of the upper and middle classes were not sent to the state schools

but obtained a better education in private schools. Nor
could the talented child of working-class origin expect to
proceed to the higher levels of education by means of scholarships, for there were virtually none available to him. Only
by making his fortune in industry or trade, or by emigrating,
could an English working man hope to escape from his position
of social inferiority. The Scot was better off, for Scottish
public education was of a higher standard, and there were
more university places : so that from a poor home a child
north of the Border could sometimes obtain a professional
training.

But within the working class, stamped though it was by
difference in manners and education from the 'educated
classes', there were many variations of life and behaviour.
At the top were the artisans, working at skilled trades, whether
in large factories or, more probably as yet, in small shops or
as independent men. As likely as not, an artisan would
belong to a trade union, and perhaps also to a co-operative
society and to some insurance or benefit club, which would
give him and his family a certain security against a 'rainy
day'. These men and their wives had a 'Sunday best' for
going to church or chapel, and many of them would take an
interest in national politics, carefully reading the long columns
of small print in their newspapers which reported the speeches
of Mr Gladstone or Lord Salisbury. They could afford to
have their sons apprenticed to a trade as they had been.

But this was the 'aristocracy' of the working class ; and
beneath it were millions of workers and their families who
could not depend upon a highly skilled trade. For them
unemployment or ill-health meant real destitution, for they
had no 'nest-egg' of money saved or trade-union support,
and between them and starvation lay only the charity of their
relatives and neighbours or the harsh discipline of the work-
house. For such folk religion probably counted for little :
they had no better clothes for Sunday wear, and in any case
could not pay the pew rents that were common in church
and chapel at this time. But only in rare cases would they
be convinced atheists, for a vague deism prevailed among
them, and Charles Bradlaugh's National Secular Society
obtained comparatively little support. Working long hours,

they were lucky if they came within the provisions of the Factory Acts, for if so they might now have a Saturday afternoon off : but they had little opportunity for recreation, and holidays at the seaside or elsewhere away from their homes were almost unheard of.

It would be difficult to generalise about working-class life as a whole, and how far it was compounded of happiness or of misery. But there can be no denying that there existed significant numbers of people living in destitution, and in conditions of housing which were far below the minimum required to maintain healthy activity. These miserable people, in total variously estimated, lived out of the sight and knowledge of the ' respectable ' people ; they had to be rediscovered by the social investigator or the socially conscious person. Andrew Mearns, a Congregational minister, wrote a little book called *The Bitter Cry of Outcast London* (1883) which led to the appointment of a Royal Commission on Housing ; and in 1884 the university settlement movement was started when Canon Barnett of St Jude's, Whitechapel, founded Toynbee Hall in memory of Arnold Toynbee. The mission work of the Salvation Army had been going on since 1878, and the Charity Organisation Society, whose object was the co-ordination of individual alms-giving, had been in action since 1869.

But there were many who felt that individual action was not enough, and that the boundaries of state activity ought to be enlarged to ensure the welfare of the people. Such persons were impelled towards ' Socialism ', though this was a word which had countless definitions. It was in fact only a tiny minority who took up with the ideas of Karl Marx, and formed a body called the Democratic Federation, later the Social-Democratic Federation (S.D.F.), to propagate their views (1881). The general reaction against the harsher forms of individualism was much wider than this—indeed, it extended to all classes of society. There were many who were attracted to the ideas of the American Henry George, who pointed to land ownership as the root of all evil, and who wanted a Single Tax on Land. What was attractive about George was not so much his remedy as his diagnosis of the evils of the social system, and his belief that something could be done about them.

In many ways, therefore, this was a moment of new beginnings in social thought. People were no longer entirely happy either about the progress of industrial development or about the merits of the society that it was creating. Samuel Smiles's *Self-Help* (1859), popular though it still was, could no longer be the Bible of the new era ; the younger generation started out from Henry George's *Progress and Poverty* (1879), and often moved on from there to examine the problems of industry. The same restlessness infected literature in general : the same contrast of outlook is to be found, for instance, between the *Autobiography* of Anthony Trollope (1883), whose smooth descriptions of country-house society had long dominated the market for novels, and the works of the social novelists of the middle 1880's, such as George Gissing. In other fields of artistic endeavour there was an attempt to escape from the harsh reality of contemporary life into aestheticism (as in the critical work of Walter Pater) or into medievalism (as in William Morris's craftsmanship and poetry). Owing to the invention of photography, painting had long since reacted against an exaggerated realism, and had found new directions in Impressionism, introduced to Britain by Whistler. Political philosophy moved, not unnaturally, away from the individualism of the early John Stuart Mill into the more positive view of state powers which we associate with T. H. Green and the Idealists (the popularity of Herbert Spencer's ' laissez-faire ' ideas was largely in the United States). And religious thought, reacting both against the new scientific theories of Darwin and Huxley and against the grim realities of contemporary social problems, found refuge in sacramentalism. But books on religion now had less interest for the general reader, who was turning increasingly to social and economic subjects : a sign of the times.

2 The Era of Imperialism
1886-1901

IN THE last fifteen years of the nineteenth century British
trade experienced better conditions, broken only by a bad
spell in 1892–4. The gradual decline of prices, which had
been taking place ever since 1873, ended about the middle of
the 1890's with the influx of gold from the new discoveries in
South Africa ; and with this the ' Great Depression ' may be
regarded as having at last come to an end. An increased
impetus was given to investment and to the expansion of
trade in Africa, Australasia, Canada, and South America ;
and although the firm of Barings, which had been speculating
too deeply in South American promotions, collapsed suddenly
in 1890, the general picture was one of successful activity in
the overseas money market.

All this meant short-term profits for British investors, but
heavy overseas investment was really a diversion from an
object of great national importance, namely the re-equipment
of British home industry to meet the challenge of its competitors. For the rivalry of the other industrial powers continued to grow. The McKinley tariff of the United States,
introduced in 1890, was particularly damaging to the export
of textiles ; and even the British colonies in Australasia had
begun to impose duties on imports from Britain. Alternative
markets in the rest of the world did not suffice to keep up the
level of textile exports, although they remained the largest
items by value in the total inventory of goods sent overseas.
At the same time it was significant that the export of British
machinery made rapid progress in these years, for this
machinery was likely to be used to increase the competition
with Britain in the future. Even more remarkable was the
amount of coal that now went abroad : the number of miners

14

in Britain rose from 382,000 in 1881 to 644,000 in 1901, and the value of coal exports rose from about £8 million to £38 million. But this in itself was an indication of the growth of foreign industry, which demanded the use of coal for its factories. And even the considerable expansion of the British coal output was being surpassed elsewhere : American production, although almost entirely consumed at home, was nevertheless in excess of British production by 1900. The British iron and steel industry, which had by 1886 already fallen to second place behind the United States', was by 1900 well behind Germany's also ; while the American industry by 1900 was more than twice as large as the British.

Lack of investment in home industry seems to account for the comparatively limited structural changes that took place, in spite of heavy foreign competition. As might be expected under such circumstances, there was some tendency to form amalgamations, such as the United Alkali Company (1891) which brought together a number of firms in the chemical industry, and the English Sewing-Cotton Company (1897), and the Bradford Dyers Association (1898). But on the whole alliances and federations of employers were more common than amalgamations. One motive for the closer co-operation of firms in the same trades was provided by the growing strength of trade unions, some of which were now of national significance ; this was a threat that only combination on the part of the employers could deal with effectively, as was shown by the struggle of the Engineering Employers' Federation against the Amalgamated Society of Engineers in the national strike of 1897-8. But a more important motive was provided by the fact that the competition from abroad came from firms of great size and strength—from German ' cartels ' and from American ' trusts ' or combines. The tendency towards amalgamation in the United States accelerated in these years, and reached a climax, in the view of British observers, in 1901. In that year people in Britain not only heard with astonishment of the formation of the United States Steel Corporation, with a capital of ' a billion dollars ' ; they also became alarmed by the acquisition by American interests of the Leyland shipping line and of Ogdens Ltd, the tobacco firm. In the latter case, the immediate result was the consolidation of most of the remaining British tobacco firms into the Imperial Tobacco Company. It was no wonder that some people began to speak of ' the Americanisation of the world ' : this in fact was the title of a sensational work by the enterprising journalist W. T. Stead. At the same time more thought began to be given to the problems of industrial efficiency in Britain, and the American and German patterns of technical education, management, and salesmanship began to receive attention.

Of equal significance was the failure of British industry to pioneer the application of new inventions or the development of new industries. The leadership of Germany in chemicals and of the United States in the electrical industry has already been mentioned. In this period it was remarkable how many of the new methods of improved transport were being exploited in foreign countries. In shipbuilding, it is true, Britain remained in the forefront, and the Parsons marine turbine was a British invention. But it was the German, Gottfried Daimler, who in 1885-6 patented the high-speed internal-combustion engine ; and it was the Frenchman, Levasseur, whose Panhard car initiated the automobile industry. Restrictive legislation to some extent hindered Britain here : it was not until 1896 that power-driven vehicles were permitted on the roads without a man walking in front and carrying a red flag. The electric tram, which began to make its appearance in Britain in the 1890's, was developed first both in Germany and in the United States, and much more slowly in Britain. Not infrequently now British industries had to turn to America for the machinery to bring them up to date ; for instance for typewriters, for new printing equipment (the Linotype), and for shoe-manufacturing machines.

Meanwhile the condition of agriculture went from bad to worse. Wheat prices still further declined, and the acreage of wheat-fields in Britain in 1900 was not much more than half what it had been in 1872. A further Royal Commission on Agriculture deliberated on the problem for four years from 1893, but could only recommend tinkering reforms. In the meantime farmers were increasingly driven off their land, except for those of them who found a certain refuge in the increasing market for fresh vegetables and dairy produce;

and the number of agricultural labourers rapidly diminished
—by 18 per cent in the decade of the 1890's alone.

With such a situation of rivalry in industrial markets, it is
not surprising that many Britons turned eagerly to the remoter,
less developed territories of the world, in some of which there
was still opportunity for the extension of political sovereignty,
and in all of which there might be mineral wealth or rich
resources of raw materials that under the new circumstances
of improved transport could make a ready profit for the
pioneer. The British Foreign Office, conscious of the limitations of the country's military strength, took a realistic view
of the possibilities of extending the bounds of the Empire.
Wherever such proposals were likely to lead to contact with a
major military power—for instance with Russia if there was
any extension in Asia—there was no diplomatic enthusiasm
for the acquisition of territory. Indeed, it had long been the
policy under these circumstances to favour the support or
even the creation of ' buffer states '—for instance Turkey,
Persia, and Afghanistan. Various powers, notably Japan,
France, and Germany, as well as Russia, were interested in
the future of China ; but it was Britain's policy, not unsuccessful in the long run, to maintain Chinese independence
and to ensure free trade in her territories. In the continent
of America, likewise, British policy came round gradually to
the recognition of the predominance of the United States,
although it needed a sharp crisis over Venezuela, which had
a boundary dispute with Britain (1895–6), to bring Lord
Salisbury's Government to a recognition of the dangers of
military intervention even in South America. There remained
the continents of Africa and Australasia ; and here, in both
cases, interest was stimulated by the discovery of gold and
other precious metals. The whole of Australia was already
British, and in 1900 it was united into the Commonwealth of
Australia ; but much of Africa, including the area of richest
mineral wealth, was either independent or disputed territory.
Here the concentration of British interest resulted in action by
colonial officials, in intense diplomacy, and finally in armed
intervention.

British interest in Africa had led, as we have seen, to the
occupation of Egypt in 1882. In 1885 a protectorate of the

Niger territories was proclaimed for the benefit of a commercial group which was chartered as the Royal Niger Company. Similarly the British East Africa Company (chartered in 1888) was associated with the extension of British rule over Kenya and Uganda, and Cecil Rhodes's British South Africa Company (1889) was responsible for the acquisition of Southern and Northern Rhodesia. This was the British share of 'the scramble for Africa', which was in fact conducted in a fairly gentlemanly way so far as the diplomacy of the major powers was concerned. German claims to territory in various parts of Africa—the Cameroons, South-West Africa, and Tanganyika—were recognised, but Zanzibar went to Britain in exchange for the small island of Heligoland, just off the North Sea coast of Germany. France's interests in Central Africa and Madagascar were also recognised.

A new phase of British interest in Africa began with the appointment of Joseph Chamberlain as Colonial Secretary in the Conservative Government of 1895. Chamberlain, a Birmingham industrialist, attached special importance to colonial affairs, and he deliberately chose to be appointed to a post which was usually regarded as one of the Cabinet offices of lesser importance. He at once brought a new sense of economic interest to bear on the problems of empire : he spoke of the British dependencies as being 'vast undeveloped estates' which required 'the judicious investment of British money'. It is still a matter of controversy how far Chamberlain was acquainted with the plans of the 'Uitlanders' or mining settlers in the Transvaal, who were anxious to overthrow the independent republic of the Boer farmers and possibly to introduce British authority into this valuable area. At any rate, he was surprised and embarrassed when one Dr Jameson, a friend of Cecil Rhodes, with the aid of a small force suddenly invaded the Transvaal at the end of 1895, apparently expecting to receive co-operation from a rising of the Uitlanders. The Uitlanders failed to rise, and the Jameson Raid ended as a fiasco ; and Chamberlain promptly disavowed any foreknowledge of it. But British public opinion, which might otherwise soon have forgotten about the incident, was roused to indignation by a telegram from the German Emperor to Kruger, the President of the Transvaal, congratulating him on preserving the independence of his country 'without appealing for the help of friendly powers '. The reaction of the Cabinet was to mobilise a ' flying squadron ' of warships capable of dealing with any foreign naval threat. This demonstration of power satisfied British public opinion for the time being.

Elsewhere in Africa conflict took place with the French, who were also probing the interior. Chamberlain organised a West African Frontier Force, consisting of Africans led by British officers, to defend British interests in West Africa against the intrusion of French expeditions and to make counter-claims. In June 1898 the two powers finally came to terms to define their respective frontiers. Things were not so easily settled in the Sudan, which Kitchener with an Egyptian army had occupied after heavy slaughter of the ' dervishes ' at Omdurman in September 1898. Kitchener found a small French force installed at Fashoda, on the White Nile. A serious diplomatic struggle at once developed, the British Foreign Office demanding French withdrawal and the French Government at first refusing to give way. After some months of deadlock, when the two countries seemed to be on the brink of war, the French finally gave way and agreed that French troops should withdraw behind the watershed of the Nile and the Congo (March 1899).

Meanwhile the situation in South Africa remained unresolved. Kruger, fearing the worst, embarked on a costly programme of armaments ; the Uitlanders continued to protest at their treatment at the hands of the Boers. After an incident in Johannesburg involving the death of a British workman, the British Government decided to demand some concessions by the Boers, preferably the granting of the Transvaal franchise to the Uitlanders who were still regarded as foreigners. Protracted negotiations took place between Kruger and the British High Commissioner in South Africa, Sir Alfred Milner, in which neither showed much adroitness ; and in September both sides started moving troops. Early in October the Boers delivered an ultimatum demanding the withdrawal of British reinforcements ; and on its rejection the two Boer republics (for the Transvaal was supported by the Orange Free State) declared war and sent their troops to invade British territory.

The war that followed began with spectacular setbacks for the British forces, whose leaders, trained in warfare against primitive tribesmen, did not know how to deal with the skilled Boer sharpshooters. The Boer armies were soon besieging a number of British towns—Mafeking in Bechuanaland, where Colonel Robert Baden-Powell was in charge, Kimberley, just inside the border of Cape Colony, and Ladysmith in Natal. To deal with the situation an army corps of some 50,000 troops was hastily mobilised in Britain and sent out under General Sir Redvers Buller. Buller unwisely divided this force so as to relieve the pressure both at Kimberley and in Natal. Hampered by poor information, both sections of the force suffered serious reverses in December : Methuen, *en route* for Kimberley, was defeated at Magersfontein and Buller in Natal suffered heavy losses at Colenso.

The reaction in Britain was immediate : it recognised that a major military campaign had to be faced. The Government decided to send out at once the ablest and most experienced commanders—Lord Roberts as Commander-in-Chief, and Kitchener, now Lord Kitchener of Khartoum, as Chief of Staff. A new army was built up, consisting of reservists, militia, and newly raised yeomanry and volunteer service units. The yeomanry were mounted infantry, for which there was an obvious need in South Africa : they were to copy the Boer tactics of rapid movement followed by rapid shooting from positions on the ground. Many of them were recruited from colonial sources—from Canada, Australia, and New Zealand, and from Natal and the Cape Colony.

In January Buller suffered a further defeat at Spion Kop, largely due to his own hesitant leadership. But the tide now began to turn. In February Roberts moved rapidly forward and in a few days General French with a cavalry force was able to relieve Kimberley. This advance resulted in the isolation and capture of a large Boer force under General Cronje. Early in March Buller at last raised the siege of Ladysmith, and Roberts rapidly occupied Bloemfontein, the capital of the Orange Free State. After being held up for several weeks by an epidemic of enteric fever among his troops, Roberts moved forward to the invasion of the Transvaal in May. On his left flank the defenders of Mafeking,

Plate 1 QUEEN VICTORIA IN 1885

Plate 2 SCENES OF THE 1890's. (*Above*) A flower seller in the City of London.
(*Below*) On the beach at Southsea.

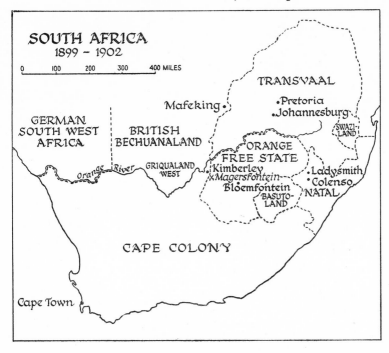

who had behaved with great gallantry under Baden-Powell's
inspiring leadership, were relieved on 17th May. Johannesburg was taken on 31st May and Pretoria fell on 5th June.
The Boer forces were now largely broken up, and it seemed
that an early conclusion to the war was at hand. But this
was not to be : Christian De Wet organised guerrilla warfare
which secured a number of irritating successes at the expense
of the British troops, and Roberts introduced a policy of
farm-burning in order to weaken the invisible enemy. This
was the position when, late in 1900, Roberts was ordered
home, leaving Kitchener to supervise the mopping-up operations. Kitchener methodically swept the country, fencing off
large areas and then sending masses of troops to search them
for the enemy. De Wet and many of his troops survived all
through 1901, and even mounted raids on the Cape Colony ;
but early in 1902 their situation became very difficult. On
31st May 1902 the remaining Boer leaders surrendered their
independence at the Peace of Vereeniging.

(2,274)   3

So ended the South African War. Judged by the number of British casualties, it was not an affair of very great national importance : less than 8,000 soldiers were killed, although there were another 13,000 who died of sickness and accident. But it woke the population of Britain to a number of significant features of the new era : the isolation of Britain among the great powers, all of whom, with the partial exception of the United States, sympathised with the Boers ; the loyalty of the self-governing colonies, which contributed so many troops to the British side ; and perhaps most of all, the insufficiency of the existing peace-time army, which had shown itself incapable of dealing with the situation, though incautiously optimistic at the outset. The importance of the war for domestic politics we shall discuss later, after outlining the course of political events from 1885.

★

Right from the start of the period domestic politics in Britain reflected the growing interest in imperial expansion ; but at first the dominant issue was one affecting the British Isles themselves—the question of whether or not the union of Great Britain and Ireland should be preserved. The force of Irish nationalism was partly due to the extension of democracy, partly also as we have seen to the agricultural depression, which had a far worse effect on a country where half the population was directly dependent on the soil for its upkeep —for Britain the figure was less than 14 per cent.

The 1885 general election brought the Irish question to the forefront of British politics, for Parnell and his supporters held the balance of power in the House of Commons. Gladstone accepted the need for Home Rule, but at first tried to keep his conviction secret, in the hope that the Conservative Government would propose a measure to which Liberal support could be given. Unfortunately an indiscretion by his son Herbert revealed his new attitude, and Conservative opinion hardened against any such course. In any case it did not seem that Lord Salisbury, who had opposed previous ' surrenders ' by his party—such as that over franchise reform in 1867—was the man to behave like Peel, who had accepted free trade in 1846. In January 1886 the Conservative Government was defeated in the Commons and resigned ; and in February Gladstone took office once more.

When Gladstone sought to work out the details of a Home Rule Bill, he was at once faced with dissension among his colleagues. He had consulted them but little about his plans ; and some of them, notably the Radical leader Chamberlain, had grown impatient at this treatment. Their disapproval centred on Gladstone's proposal to remove the Irish M.P.s from Westminster altogether, which would have effectively destroyed the remnant of central control. At the same time his scheme allowed for the Westminster Parliament continuing to tax Ireland for ' imperial ' purposes—i.e. defence, debt interest, etc. Gladstone had clearly made a mistake in recommending the exclusion of Irish members from Westminster, though it was almost equally difficult to see how their participation there could be limited to ' imperial ' questions. At any rate, the Bill was attacked both by Chamberlain and a band of his Radical supporters, and by Hartington, backed by a large number of Whigs. In June Gladstone's proposals were decisively beaten in the House of Commons by 343 votes to 313 : 93 Liberals, most of them Whigs, had voted with the majority.

Under these circumstances Gladstone decided to dissolve. His policy had met with the approval of the National Liberal Federation, which thus parted from its creator, Joseph Chamberlain, whose support was virtually limited to the Birmingham Association. Gladstone also now had the firm alliance of the Irish Nationalists under Parnell. But there was a marked swing away from the Liberal Party in the election, especially in England. 316 Conservatives were returned, together with 78 dissentient Liberals who opposed Home Rule ; the Gladstonian Liberals numbered only 191, and there were 85 Irish Nationalists. Gladstone at once resigned, and Salisbury formed a Conservative ministry dependent on the support of the dissentient Liberals.

From this point onwards the political situation became more stable, and consequently was less eventful. The new accession of strength to the Conservative Party occasioned by the Home Rule issue enabled Salisbury to pay less attention to the Radical wing of his own party : and when in December Randolph Churchill, who had become Chancellor of the Exchequer, resigned on a budgetary question—he thought that the military estimates were too high—Salisbury could readily replace him with the former Liberal financier G. J. Goschen.   Churchill's reported comment, 'I forgot Goschen', was symbolical of a new situation in which the 'Tory democracy' that he stood for was no longer indispensable to Salisbury.   Salisbury's nephew, Arthur Balfour, became Chief Secretary of Ireland in 1887 and provided the effective Commons leadership that the Government needed.   Salisbury's position was further consolidated by the Queen's jubilee celebrations of 1887 and by the 'Pigott forgeries', documents which were published by *The Times* and which, though later proved to be false, put Parnell under suspicion of planning violent outrages.   Although Parnell finally emerged unblemished from this case, he was even more discredited, in accordance with the morality of the time, by being involved as a 'guilty party' in the O'Shea divorce case which took place in 1890.   Shocking as it was to the 'nonconformist conscience', this case led Gladstone to demand Parnell's resignation as leader of the Irish Party.   Parnell refused to give way, but he was supported by less than half of his parliamentary party, which thereupon fell into two bitterly disputing factions.

Under these circumstances the Government could turn its attention to other questions than Ireland ; and an overdue reform of local government was now undertaken and passed into law in 1888.   County councils were created, at least one for each existing county, and also one for London which was carved out of Middlesex, Surrey, and Kent.   Then in 1891 school fees in elementary schools were at last abolished, and a new Factory Act raised the minimum age for the employment of children to eleven.

Meanwhile the Liberal Party had been to some extent recouping its strength.   The loss of Whigs and Chamberlain Radicals left it more than ever a party of the 'Celtic fringe', and this was plainly evident in the so-called 'Newcastle Programme' which the National Liberal Federation adopted at its conference at Newcastle in the autumn of 1891.   Home

Rule for Ireland and Church disestablishment in Wales and Scotland were the chief points in the programme, although there were also proposals designed to appeal to various other interest groups—employers' liability legislation for the trade unionists, land reform for the rural voters, and local veto for the temperance enthusiasts.   The Liberal Party machine had now been consolidated with the transfer of the headquarters of the National Liberal Federation from Birmingham to London, where they were housed in the same building as the Whips' office.

In 1892 Salisbury dissolved Parliament, and the Liberals fought the election so far as they could on the basis of their whole programme of reforms, but Ireland was again the principal issue for the voters.   The Liberals recovered some ground and won 273 seats, as against 269 for the Conservatives and 46 for the Liberal Unionists, as the supporters of Chamberlain and Hartington were called.   The Irish Nationalists numbered 81, and there was a single Independent Labour member—Keir Hardie, a Scottish miner.   The result gave a small majority to Home Rule, but it was a very unevenly distributed majority : Ireland and Wales were predominantly in favour, but England was still opposed.   Under these somewhat doubtful omens Gladstone again took office.

The new Prime Minister was now 82—rather unkindly described by Queen Victoria as ' an old, wild, and incomprehensible man ', deriving his strength only from his passionate determination to deal with the Irish question.   This time his Home Rule Bill had been more carefully drawn up : a committee of leading Liberals had deliberated over its clauses, and they had decided to maintain the representation of Ireland at Westminster, although the Irish members were to be allowed to vote only on matters of Irish or imperial concern.   The Bill, introduced in early 1893, was passed through the Commons by a narrow margin after long debates, but it was defeated in the Lords in September by a majority of 419 to 41.   Gladstone now wished to dissolve again, but his Cabinet refused to support him in this course ; he also found himself in the minority in opposing increased naval expenditure.   In March 1894 he therefore resigned ; and Queen Victoria, glad to be rid of him and scorning to consult him about a successor, chose the young Whig aristocrat, Lord Rosebery.

Deprived of their great leader Gladstone, and hampered by the highly partisan activity of the Lords, there was little that the Liberals could now do. An Act establishing parish councils had been passed just before Gladstone retired ; but afterwards hardly anything of note occurred except that the Prime Minister's horse won the Derby in both 1894 and 1895. The one memorable political change was the introduction of death duties in Harcourt's budget of 1894—a measure that was to have great social significance in the future, but which owed its introduction at this time to the need to raise revenue for the naval building programme. But for the time being the highest rate of contribution was 8 per cent. On this occasion, as often, social change inside Britain was due more to her external situation than to purely domestic considerations.

In June 1895 Rosebery resigned after being defeated in a snap vote in the Commons ; Salisbury formed a minority government—a coalition with the Liberal Unionists, in which Hartington, now Duke of Devonshire, and Chamberlain both took office. Salisbury soon dissolved, and the succeeding general election gave him a majority of 152 : there were 340 Conservatives and 71 Liberal Unionists as against 177 Liberals and 82 Irish Nationalists. The one Independent Labour member, Keir Hardie, had been defeated ; but the party that he had formed, the Independent Labour Party, had put up altogether 28 candidates, and although all of them were defeated their intervention in some cases resulted in the defeat of the Liberals. However, a more important cause of Liberal defeat was the rising tide of imperialism, which resulted from emotions aroused by the ' scramble for Africa ' which we have already examined.

In the new Unionist Government Salisbury was both Prime Minister and Foreign Secretary ; Balfour was Leader in the Commons ; and it would have seemed very much of a family government if it had not been for the strong personality of Chamberlain, who deliberately chose the minor office of Colonial Secretary for the exercise of his talents. Chamberlain was keen to see the Government take positive measures in the social sphere, but his imperial commitments prevented very much being done. The most important measure was the Workmen's Compensation Act of 1897, which provided many workers with compensation for industrial accidents. Chamberlain was also anxious to see the enactment of a scheme for old-age pensions, but after successive committees had examined the problem the whole idea had to be shelved owing to the heavy expense of the South African War.

The end of the century thus saw the major questions of social reform being subordinated to the problems of empire. By the time of the outbreak of the South African War, even the Liberal Party had many advocates of imperialism in its ranks. Rosebery, who had resigned the leadership of the party in 1896, was one of these ; and others were H. H. Asquith, R. B. Haldane, and Edward Grey. Ranged against them were the ' Gladstonians ', faithful to the ' little England ' attitude of their revered leader who died in May 1898— notably John Morley, Herbert Gladstone, and the young Welsh leader David Lloyd George. Sir Henry Campbell-Bannerman, who accepted the party leadership when Asquith refused it on grounds of poverty in 1898, happened to lie somewhere between the two wings of the party, which without his presence might well have altogether fallen apart at the end of the century. As it was, the Liberal Imperialists, or ' Limps ', got to the stage of forming their own organisation, the Liberal League, which sponsored candidatures and did its best to thwart the ' little Englanders ', or ' pro-Boers ' as they were also called.

The ' pro-Boers ', who were only a section of their own party, were in the awkward situation of standing against the full force of popular enthusiasm for the South African War. They held that the war in South Africa was the fault of the British Government and should never have been undertaken. Their appearances at public meetings frequently caused rioting, and it required considerable courage for them to continue to express their views. Most prominent among them was Lloyd George, who first won general notice at this time. In 1901 he even dared to address a meeting of the South African Conciliation Committee—the ' pro-Boer ' propaganda body— in the city of Birmingham, Chamberlain's preserve : in the midst of serious disturbances he escaped only by disguising himself as a police constable.

But if the South African War divided the Liberals, it secured unity among the Irish, who since 1890 had been divided into Parnellites and anti-Parnellites. The Conservative policy towards Ireland had been one of ' killing Home Rule by kindness ', and Balfour as Chief Secretary had carried a useful Land Purchase Act, which had gone some way to appease the peasantry. For some time, therefore, the flame of Irish nationalism seemed to be burning low. But in 1898 a new body, the United Irish League, was formed by William O'Brien, an anti-Parnellite, as an instrument of agrarian agitation, but also with the purpose of fusing the rival elements of the movement. This purpose was accomplished early in 1900, a few months after the war had broken out.

Another body which came into existence just as the Irish were reuniting was the Labour Representation Committee, which was later to be the Labour Party. It was founded at a meeting of delegates of trade unions and Socialist societies, which had been summoned as the result of a resolution of the 1899 T.U.C. The resolution was largely the work of the Independent Labour Party, the body led by Keir Hardie. The I.L.P. had been unsuccessful on its own at the 1895 General Election, but it developed the policy of collaborating with other Socialist bodies and above all with the organised trade unions, which by now were well enough off to sponsor political activity if they wished. It need not be supposed that more than a few of the union leaders had been converted to Socialism : their motive in entering the political sphere was primarily to safeguard themselves against the political influence of employers' organisations, the strength of which had become obvious at the time of the engineers' strike in 1897-8. Nor did the formation of the new party create much of a stir : it happened to coincide with the relief of Ladysmith and the capture of the Boer general Cronje ; and the newspapers naturally had little room for domestic events, especially such a one as this, which seemed to hold little importance for the immediate future. There can have been few who guessed that the first secretary of the Labour Representation Committee, a young man called Ramsay MacDonald, would later become Prime Minister as the leader of this same organisation.

In the summer of 1900, with the campaign in South Africa apparently drawing to a victorious close, the Government decided to appeal to the country. The Liberals were still deeply divided ; and the Labour Representation Committee could put only fifteen candidates into the field. It was natural, therefore, that there should have been an easy win for the Conservatives. They did not, however, do as well as in 1895 : then they had had a majority of 152 ; but losses at by-elections had reduced this to 128, and now they returned with a majority of 134. Wales, which naturally inclined to a ' little England ' policy, went more strongly Liberal than before ; and even in some of the English cities there were Liberal gains. Two of the candidates of the L.R.C. were returned, including Keir Hardie who as a ' pro-Boer ' profited by the fact that he was opposing a Liberal imperialist in a Welsh constituency.

★

The last years of the nineteenth century saw a continued rapid growth in the British population : it rose from under 30 million in 1881 to 37 million in 1901 ; and if Ireland were included, the total now exceeded that of France. But the Irish population was decreasing, as it had done since the middle of the century : in 1881 it was 5·1 million, and twenty years later it was down to 4·3 million. The discrepancy between Britain and Ireland was in large part due to migration : that from Britain was now slackening, for in the 1890's it amounted to an annual average of less than 110,000, of whom a majority continued to go to the United States.

Although the population of Britain was still rapidly rising, significant changes were beginning to take place in the size of families : the upper and middle classes were now practising birth-control, and parents restricted themselves to two or three children. Only in the working class were families of up to ten children still common. The houses that were built for the new middle-class families in the suburbs could be smaller, more compact, and so less expensive. The savings that the smaller families occasioned could be devoted to some of the new luxuries of life—holidays at the seaside, bicycles, and perhaps even at the end of the century a motor car, though these were at first very expensive.

More and more it was this suburban middle class which set the tone of British life. The old aristocracy still existed at the apex of society, but its dependence on the countryside steadily declined as agriculture became less and less profitable. Men like Chamberlain and Goschen rose to political supremacy in the company of many other members of their own class : it was a very marked feature of ' Liberal Unionism ' that so many of its M.P.s were business men. They demanded efficiency in government, and were keen advocates of greater powers for local authorities, so that business might have a background of efficiently operated local services. Chamberlain himself as Mayor of Birmingham in the 1870's had done much to extend municipal powers in the sphere of gas and water supplies and other amenities : this period saw the extension of these ideas, sometimes called municipal Socialism, to many other cities including London, where with the creation of the London County Council it became possible for a group of ' Progressives ' (an alliance that ran through the political spectrum from Conservatives to Socialists) to apply ideas akin to Chamberlain's on an even larger scale.

These improvements benefited all classes of the population ; and the advance of the working class as a whole was also much furthered by the gradual decline of prices, which came to an end only in the later 1890's. Real wages appear to have risen in this period by something like 40 per cent on the average. It is true that the sharp depressions of 1886-7 and 1893-4 caused much unemployment, which led to great misery at a time when there was no unemployment pay. In 1886 and 1887 there was sporadic rioting in London, which attracted special notice because it took place in connection with meetings of the little Socialist groups of the metropolis. H. M. Hyndman's body, the S.D.F., and William Morris's Socialist League which was an offshoot from it, constantly urged the cause of ' social revolution '. But Socialism did not ' catch on ' with the working class at this time, and the Socialist groups which sought working-class support proved to be less important than the more academic thinkers who in 1884 formed the ' Fabian Society '. This body, tiny though it was, proved of considerable importance : it worked out a programme for the gradual attainment of Socialism by political means. Its *Fabian Essays* of 1889 were to have a profound effect in later years ; and its members, particularly Sidney Webb, played a major role in the development of the less novel ' municipal Socialism ' of this period.

The most important development for the working class at the time was probably the great extension of trade unionism among unskilled workers. A few Socialists had a part in this, and in some cases they were able to initiate the ' new unions ' as they were called ; but the movement would have been impossible without the constant improvement in working-class incomes and in literacy, which was steadily becoming universal as a result of the Education Acts. In 1888, as the country recovered from the trough of a depression, there was a successful strike by a small but significant group, the women match-workers of London. They set an example to the men of the metropolis, and soon afterwards, early in 1889, an equally successful strike of gasworkers was led by one of their number, Will Thorne, who now founded the Gasworkers and General Labourers Union. But the most notable strike of all was that of the London dockers in August and September 1889. This attracted much publicity, and ended with the concession of a wage rate of sixpence an hour, and the establishment of the Dock, Wharf, Riverside, and General Workers Union. The emphasis in the titles of the ' new unions ' on the recruitment of ' general ' workers showed that they were anxious to enrol members from all possible industries, or from none ; but in practice these ' new unions ' had to settle down to defend the interests of workers in particular trades, and so became more similar to the ' old unions ' of the skilled trades —which also expanded their membership considerably in these years. But the ' new unions ', because they could rely much less than the unions of the artisans on the bargaining power of their skill, were keen to secure legislative enactment of their demands, and so tended to support any moves for the formation of a ' labour party '. Many ' new unionists ' were prominent in the socialistic Independent Labour Party ; and the ' new unions ' were the keenest to support the efforts of this body to form a Labour Representation Committee, which as we have seen came into being in 1900. As a result of all this forming of new unions and extending of old ones, the number of trade unionists affiliated to the T.U.C. rose from half a million in 1885 to one and a quarter million in 1900, and the T.U.C.'s influence rose accordingly. Membership of co-operative societies grew in the same period from 800,000 to 1,800,000.

At the same time the working class benefited greatly from the movement of the ' social conscience ' which was already developing at the beginning of the 1880's. The rioting of . 1886 had led to a sharp increase in the Lord Mayor's Fund for the Unemployed, and some cynical observers attributed this to the intimidation of the wealthy by the poor. But the public was equally impressed, and again contributed freely, at the time of the extremely orderly dock strike : and indeed it was the orderliness of the strikers, under the control of their leaders John Burns and Tom Mann, which was most effective in winning public opinion to the strikers' side. Any sort of publicity, it seemed, was of advantage to workers, for the wealthier classes living in their more fashionable residential areas needed to be reminded of the existence of the masses of the poor in order to be moved to acts of charity. Certainly in this period the reminders were frequent : all sorts of investigations into the slums of London and other large towns were undertaken, varying from the massive scientific inquiry of Charles Booth and his colleagues in the East End to the sensational journalism of the Manchester journalist Robert Blatchford, who claimed to owe his conversion to Socialism to the conditions of misery that he discovered in Ancoats. Of the depth of the destitution there can be no doubt ; but it is also true that it received its greatest publicity just at a time when it was most rapidly on the decline. The L.C.C. and other city authorities now had powers to undertake slum clearance, and there was much done in this period. Con-siderable attention was also paid to abuses in the ' sweated ' trades, though less was done to remedy the situation : these trades were those which, owing to the small scale of their

operations, lay outside the provisions of the Factory Acts.
Among them were many of the branches of the Midland iron
trades, and also the tailoring and furniture-making of London
and Leeds, where large numbers of immigrant Jews who had
fled from the pogroms of Eastern Europe eked out a precarious
income for themselves and their families.

The passion for investigation which had spread so widely
by this time, and which was due in part to the development
of the professions, in part to the development of the press, led
to inquiries into the pattern of religious observance. In this
sphere too, what was discovered was disturbing, although it
was not a condition that was in any sense particularly novel :
it was found that by and large the workers and their families
did not go to church, and that the only services in the poorer
districts that were really well attended were those that offered
food or shelter as inducements to sugar the spiritual message.
What was novel in the situation was its recognition by church
leaders, and their willingness to do something about it, by
abolishing pew rents and by increasing the ' missions ' in the
backward districts. This was especially the case with the
Salvation Army, whose leader General William Booth was
responsible for one of the most striking works on the subject—
In Darkest England, and the Way Out (1890). But there was no
question of a religious revival being effected in this period :
the only signs of one were in Wales, where it seemed to be
closely associated with Welsh nationalism and with the hostility to the payment of tithes to the existing Establishment.
The church-going attendance of the middle class, however,
was universally high.

At a time of imperial expansion and rivalry between the
nations, there were many people who were more worried
about the efficiency of the people as workers and as soldiers
than about their moral or material welfare. Technical education was a very haphazard business until 1889, when a
Technical Instruction Act gave powers to local councils to
spend money for this purpose. An Exchequer windfall of 1890
also gave a fillip to its development ; and the Fabian leader
Sidney Webb, who was chairman of a special committee of
the L.C.C., was prominent in setting up an effective scheme
for London. Another important development was in the

growth of free libraries, ably assisted by the benefactions of Andrew Carnegie, the Scotsman who had made an enormous fortune in the American steel industry. Many public art galleries date their inception from these years, among them being the Tate Gallery and the National Portrait Gallery. For those of the middle class who could afford private education the most important development of the period was the growth of the provincial universities : in 1880 Victoria University was constituted at Manchester, and it later expanded to include colleges elsewhere ; in 1893 the University of Wales was created ; in 1900 Birmingham University. In 1898 the colleges of London were increased in number and combined into the University of London. But the annual output of graduates still remained very small.

One effect of the universal, though limited, educational system was the demand for a ' popular ' press : ' popular ' in the sense that it deliberately sought to cater for the entertainment, rather than the instruction, of the new multitudes who could afford a cheap journal. As early as 1881 George Newnes had discovered in his weekly *Tit-Bits* the sort of snappy, pre-digested news presentation which now had a wide appeal. But it took some time for daily papers to be presented in a similar way. T. P. O'Connor, who founded the London halfpenny evening paper the *Star* in 1888, was on the right lines, but he did not have the necessary business qualities to exploit his success. Eventually Alfred Harmsworth took advantage of the opportunities of the situation. After an apprenticeship in running a paper for cyclists he founded *Answers*, which was a weekly similar to *Tit-Bits*, and then, after managing a number of successful weeklies and small journals catering for special markets, and after turning the London *Evening News* into a money-maker, in 1896 he established himself once and for all with the foundation of the *Daily Mail*. This paper announced itself as ' a Penny Newspaper for a Halfpenny', and because of the brevity of its news stories, ' The Busy Man's Paper '. Within four years it was selling nearly a million copies daily—over three times as many as its largest competitor, the *Daily Telegraph*, had sold. The *Daily Mail* was run on strictly commercial lines—that is to say, it was designed to attract advertisers by securing the largest possible circulation, and to attract circulation by meeting the popular taste to the fullest possible extent. Harmsworth realised that this could be done by methods of sensationalism—by stirring up popular emotions on international issues. Undoubtedly the *Daily Mail*, with its campaigns of hostility to the French, to the Germans, and to the Boers, did much to focus the imperialist bellicosity of the period.

At the same time there were plenty of people of limited education who were not satisfied with being ' entertained ', and who were anxious above all to develop their knowledge. They were especially interested in social and economic questions : many of them, starting from Henry George, went on to study the literature of Socialism, which was amazing in its extent and variety. There was the verse and Utopian romance of William Morris, the idealistic essays of Edward Carpenter, the trenchant political utterances of Hyndman, the tracts of the Fabian Society. Yet even Socialism became ' popularised '. Its most successful individual propagandist was Robert Blatchford, whose weekly newspaper the *Clarion* secured much of its readership by setting out to entertain as well as to instruct. The *Clarion* readers were invited to join cycling clubs, glee clubs, and Cinderella clubs to help destitute children. The *Clarion* Scouts distributed copies of Blatchford's own bestseller, *Merrie England* (1894), sales of which at a penny each passed the million mark.

Harmsworth and Blatchford were both acting shrewdly in exploiting the new sport of cycling. The ' safety ' bicycle introduced in 1885 and the pneumatic tyre invented two or three years later by J. B. Dunlop were great technical advances. Since motor cars were only just appearing at the end of the period, cycling was more of a pleasure then than now. It was largely responsible for the development of less cumbrous clothing for both sexes, and to some extent for the growing uniformity of costume among all classes—though here the extension of ready-made clothing was an important factor. The lounge suit replaced the frock coat for men ; for women the bustle went out of fashion, and voluminous petticoats made way for knickers.

The ' new woman ', claiming the right to an active life, was as much a feature of the period as the new unionism or the new journalism. The Married Women's Property Act of 1893 extended a similar Act of 1882, and gave a wife as much right to her property after marriage as before. The reduction in the size of middle-class families enabled many married women to take part more fully in the life of the wider community. Both married and unmarried women were prominent in the Socialist movement—Mrs Besant was the most famous example, but there were many others. The successes of the first women to take university examinations encouraged the pioneers to further efforts : for a start they insisted on claiming the titles of degrees for which they had passed the examinations —a claim which, though virtually unanswerable, was yet formally denied to them. Even among the women of the working class the same ferment was at work, though painfully slowly as yet : there were few women trade unionists, for example, in spite of the many trades in which women worked.

All these features of the age contributed to the sense of social revolt which infected current literature. It was especially marked in drama, which began to blossom under Pinero and Henry Arthur Jones, and came to flower in the plays of Bernard Shaw. The *fin-de-siècle* movement, which found its expression in the work of Oscar Wilde and Aubrey Beardsley for the *Yellow Book*, was perhaps shaped more by Continental influences than by domestic ones, though it was notable that Wilde like Shaw was a Socialist. The novelists if not themselves Socialists were most deeply involved in social problems, as we may see from the work of the best of them such as Zangwill and Gissing. Even in architecture and the domestic arts the same sense of revolt was apparent : the influence of William Morris showed itself in a search for sincere craftsmanship and a protest against commercial values. Morris's influence on the design of wallpapers, furniture, and typography was profound. Architecture was perhaps less affected by him : but there was a marked tendency to move away from the Gothic styles which had so long been dominant, though it was in the direction of another early style—that of the English or French Renaissance.

Yet this atmosphere of social revolt among the writers and artists must not lead us to false conclusions about the main

Plate 3 THE SOUTH AFRICAN WAR. Troops storming a ' kopje ' or small hill.

Plate 4 SOCIAL UNREST. (*Above*) South Wales miners receiving strike pay in a chapel, 1910. (*Below*) Suffragettes arrested outside Buckingham Palace, 1914.

characteristics of the period. Socialism and even the idea of social reform, as we have seen, counted for little at Westminster. At the end of the century, what bulked large there, and also in the popular newspapers and on the music halls, was 'imperialism'. It was the ballads of Kipling about India, and his conception of 'the white man's burden', that caught the popular imagination. During the South African War he devoted himself to the cause of the soldiers, and collected considerable sums to spend on comforts for the wounded in the hospitals of the Cape. Kipling, indeed, was the truest embodiment of this age : the social reformers were to have their successes—in the future.

3 Social Reform and Armaments 1901-14

THE gloomy prognostications of economic disaster for Britain, which had been made at the turn of the century, did not seem to be borne out by the state of trade in the following dozen years. There were, it is true, fluctuations in employment levels, and 1904–5 in particular was a bad time ; but on the whole conditions were better than they had been in the eighties and nineties, and a fair level of employment was sustained, especially after 1910.

At the same time there were some disquieting features of the national economic situation. There was no longer any steady increase of real wages such as there had been in the later nineteenth century : for although money wages rose, there was a price inflation of a roughly equal proportion. This was evidently due in large part to a lack of capital investment in industry, which caused both a failure to expand and an inability to take up new inventions and processes. Whereas the American textile industry was making great headway with ring-spinning, the Lancashire industry made do with the old mule-spinning, which required proportionately more labour ; and while American mines were installing a great deal of coal-cutting machinery, little was done to improve the methods of mining in Britain. So too, although electric power was widely used for industrial purposes in other countries, it was little used in Britain except on Tyneside. The result was that while production might be increased by employing more labour, productivity—the output per man-hour—made little progress. An investigation of the real costs of producing cotton goods and pig iron in the period 1900–13 showed that they were still very much what they had been in the eighties ; and in the decade 1901–11, while coal pro-

duction increased 19 per cent, the labour force in the industry
had increased by 36 per cent, which argued a considerable
net loss of productivity over the period. As for agriculture,
what changes there were took place in the direction of beef
production—which meant that the minimum use was being
made of the good arable land of the country. But on the
whole agriculture changed but little.

What was the explanation of the general stagnation of the
country's industry? The country was prosperous, by all
previous standards, and yet it was not advancing. There
seemed to be plenty of capital available, but it was not being
used to increase the output of industry. The explanation is
that in increasing quantities it was going abroad. The rapid
improvements in transport facilities in the previous generation
had opened up unusually profitable opportunities in new and
distant lands, many of them being inside the British Empire.
The increase in the number of persons emigrating from Britain
gives some clue to this fresh activity : in the first ten years of
the century one and a half million Britons left the United
Kingdom to make their homes abroad, and 56 per cent of
them (double the proportion of the previous decade) went to
lands within the Empire. In the years after 1910 the flow
increased to a quarter of a million each year, yet again the
proportion going to Empire lands increased. Canada, Australia,
New Zealand, and the newly pacified South Africa were the
principal recipients of these migrants ; their populations
rapidly shot up, and the exploitation of their resources developed in proportion. Capital from Britain was urgently needed
for railway building in the new lands ; and with such an
increase of potential customers the return on the capital was
sure to be excellent. The opening of new farming lands in
the Canadian prairies and the expansion of Australasian sheep
farming demanded British capital, just as did the development
of the gold mines in South Africa. Nor was it only to the
Empire countries that British capital freely flowed : enter-
prises in the United States, in South America, and as far
afield as Japan all benefited from the willingness of the British
investor to seek out the most lucrative opportunities.

Thus it was that the efficiency of British home industry,
busy as it was, made no marked forward progress. Old

machinery continued in use, while foreign competitors were making rapid replacements. New industries were built up only slowly : as late as 1913, for instance, more motor cars and car parts were being imported than exported. There was a much increased demand abroad for British coal, but this was only so that foreign countries could make their own manufactures. The only major industry in which British predominance seemed virtually unchallengeable was ship-building, where as late as 1910–14 Britain produced 61·9 per cent of the world's total tonnage.

It was natural that controversy should develop on the causes of Britain's comparative stagnation ; unfortunate, however, that it should be diverted from the fundamental problems of technical efficiency to the political tangles of the fiscal question. It was true, of course, that Britain's principal competitors in world markets, Germany and the United States, were heavily protected on their home markets, and that in addition the Germans had the advantage of elaborate state subsidies and rebates. But it was by no means clear that British industry as a whole would benefit on balance from the imposition of tariffs ; and the leader of the Tariff Reform campaign, Joseph Chamberlain, had various political motives in mind in making his proposals—the most important of which was that a system of preference or free trade for imperial goods inside a protected area would help to knit the Empire together and perhaps provide the basis for a federal system under the Crown, just as the *Zollverein* had helped to unite Germany into an Imperial Federation.

Chamberlain's proposals, as he expounded them in 1903, were not readily acceptable to his colleagues in the Government, and he was forced to carry on his campaign as a private citizen instead of as the Colonial Secretary. But such was the force of his oratory, and such the support that he received from at least a large proportion of industry and from a large section of the Conservative Party, that Tariff Reform became the major political issue of the country for several years. In the first two decades of the century, however, it could fairly be said that the bulk of the electorate preferred to stick to the established system of free trade. There were at the time a good many sound reasons for this. Although trade with

Empire lands was increasing rapidly, so was trade with foreign countries, which remained in total value a much larger proportion of all British exports. There was the danger that tariffs would lead to a considerable price increase at home, especially for food and other essential goods. And then there was the difficulty that some of the Empire countries were beginning to take an interest in building up their own industries against Britain, while at the same time wishing to preserve their own agricultural export markets with foreign countries. At the 1907 Colonial Conference, for instance, it was obvious that no scheme such as Chamberlain proposed would commend itself to the Canadian Government, which was pursuing a policy of political and economic independence. Although it was decided at this conference to meet regularly in the future every four years, under the new title ' Imperial Conference ', there was strong opposition to proposals for the establishment of a permanent secretariat or for the conversion of the conference into an ' Imperial Council '.

The policy of the new Liberal Government in Britain was in any case hostile to Chamberlain's ideas for closer integration of the Empire : its leaders were prepared to encourage the trend towards autonomy in the English-speaking colonies, now especially well developed in Canada and Australasia. In particular they favoured the establishment of a Union of South Africa, including the former Boer republics, and this finally came into existence in 1910 with powers not dissimilar from those enjoyed by the other self-governing colonies or ' Dominions ', as they were officially known after the 1907 Colonial Conference. The establishment of the Union of South Africa was a remarkable gesture of trust in a defeated enemy, but in the short run it was justified by the generous response that it evoked from the Boer leaders Botha and Smuts. By the Indian Councils Act of 1909 the Liberal Government also began cautiously to develop the provincial legislative councils of India, so that they began to assume the characteristics of genuinely representative bodies.

By the end of the first decade of the twentieth century, however, Britain's anxiety about the problems of defence began to take priority over all other considerations. This was largely because of the growth of the German Empire and the threat to

British security that was posed by the growth of the German fleet. In the nineteenth century Britain had long regarded France and Russia as the powers that most threatened her world position ; but the rapid rise of Germany made her diplomatists recognise, as Salisbury put it, that she had ' backed the wrong horse '. The South African War had shown the perils of isolation ; and it was obvious that Britain could not single-handed face a world combination of powers, if that should come about. In 1902 Lord Lansdowne, the Foreign Secretary, negotiated a treaty of alliance with Japan, which was to operate if either country were involved in war with more than one other great power. This guaranteed Japan, which anticipated war with Russia, against the intervention of France ; and it guaranteed Britain, which still thought of France as a major rival, against having to face the fleets of both France and Russia at the same time, without any naval ally.

Anglo-Japanese Pact

But now the situation was changing rapidly in Europe. Delcassé, the French Foreign Minister, was eager to conciliate Britain so as to secure support against Germany and Austria ; and Lansdowne realised that there was much to be said for at least an adjustment of the many outstanding differences between Britain and France. These differences were principally about Africa : Britain challenged the French claim to predominance in Morocco, and France had always resented the British control of Egypt. Under the agreement of 1904— the *entente cordiale* as it was called—Britain undertook to support France in Morocco, and the French undertook to support British policy in Egypt. This agreement freed Britain from the need, constantly felt ever since 1882, to win German support for her Egyptian policy, which could easily be embarrassed by the united opposition of the great powers. Delcassé rightly calculated that this would encourage Britain to pursue a policy much less friendly to Germany.

But this did not mean that Britain was now regarding Germany as a potential enemy. The *entente* was not an alliance : indeed, it was at first no more than a *détente*—an arrangement for the relaxation of tension between Britain and France. That it became more than this in a short time was due much more to other developments in the pattern of international relations. One was the rapid growth of the

German Navy, which caused the Admiralty to decide to concentrate the British fleet in home waters, and led to pressure for closer ties with France so as to guarantee the safety of the Mediterranean.   Another was the Russo-Japanese war of 1904–5, which convinced Britain of the weakness of Russia and so led her to regard Germany as dangerously close to European predominance.   And a third was the fact of direct German intervention in Morocco in 1905, which brought the terms of the *entente* into early operation and thereby obliged Britain to give direct diplomatic support to France.   An international conference was summoned to Algeciras early in 1906 to reconcile these competing claims, and Germany, deprived of all help from other powers save Austria-Hungary, was obliged to give way.

Sir Edward Grey, the Foreign Secretary of the Liberal Government which took office at the end of 1905, was himself a Liberal Imperialist, and he saw no reason to disagree with the general policy of his Conservative predecessors.   In 1907 he made an agreement with Russia for the removal of differences, and this was similar in form to the agreement with France : it concerned frontier differences in Persia, Afghanistan, and Tibet.   But the settlement of these questions involved no undertakings for mutual support, and since the new British Government was anxious to cut its expenditure on armaments, it also made approaches to Germany in the hope of securing some sort of disarmament agreement.   Nothing came of this : but Grey continued to take a position quite independent of Russia, as was evident in the Balkans crisis of 1908.

At this point, however, public opinion in Britain began to be seriously concerned about the progress of the country's naval rearmament.   The new battleship *Dreadnought* (completed in 1907) made all other battleships obsolete ; but Germany was rapidly laying down ships of this type.   To make sure of keeping well ahead of Germany, an immediate programme to construct eight new ' dreadnoughts ' seemed to be required ; and a popular agitation, summed up in the slogan ' We want eight and we won't wait,' persuaded the Government to accept this in spite of opposition from social reformers, who had other plans for any surplus revenue.

Meanwhile R. B. Haldane, as Secretary for War, had

initiated a far-reaching modernisation of the Army. He established a general staff, formed an expeditionary force suitable for immediate overseas service in the event of war, and merged the non-regular forces into one new body, the Territorial Force. All this he managed to do while the military budget was being heavily cut under Radical pressure. The Committee of Imperial Defence, a standing committee of the Cabinet which had been set up in 1902 as a result of the South African War, now acquired greater importance as the need for planning military and naval action in concert, and for associating the Dominions with such action if possible, became more and more obvious. In 1911, when Winston Churchill became First Lord of the Admiralty, a naval staff was established there to parallel the army staff, and the plans of the two services were co-ordinated.

The changes in the defence structure made in 1911 were prompted by a fresh crisis in international affairs, which arose from an abrupt intervention by Germany in Morocco. A German gunboat was sent to the Moroccan port of Agadir, evidently with the intention of securing for Germany some compensation for the complete French absorption of the country. Lloyd George, who was the leading social reformer in the British Cabinet, gave a solemn warning that no government could stand for Britain being treated ' as if she were of no account in the cabinet of nations ' ; and this seems to have forced the German Foreign Office to recognise that Britain was again giving strong diplomatic support to France. It was not, however, until October that an agreement was made whereby Germany was provided with compensation in the Congo for France's acquisition of Morocco.

After this crisis a further attempt was made to secure a *détente* with Germany, and Haldane visited Berlin for conversations : but these foundered on the German insistence that Britain should pledge herself to neutrality under all circumstances involving Germany in war. The concentration of the British Navy in home waters, and of the French Navy in the Mediterranean, was effected more completely than ever, and no verbal disavowal of an Anglo-French military alliance, such as was made in 1912 by an exchange of letters between Grey and the French ambassador, could conceal the importance of this.

In 1912 the main scene of international rivalry shifted to the Balkans, where the weakness of Turkish power provoked a rising in Albania and then a joint war against Turkey by Bulgaria, Serbia, Greece, and Montenegro. In view of the threat to European peace involved in any change in the Balkan *status quo*, Grey acted to secure a settlement of the conflict by an ambassadors' conference in London. His efforts were at first successful, but in 1913 war was resumed when the victorious powers fell out among themselves, and Rumania also intervened. The upshot was to strengthen Rumania, Serbia, and Greece at the expense of Bulgaria and Turkey. These changes, particularly the increase in the size of Serbia, were especially embarrassing to Austria-Hungary, which had a considerable Slav minority within its borders. While for the time being the Austro-Hungarian Government appeared to accept the situation, it became obvious within a year that it had not done so.

Thus, although Grey worked hard to conciliate Germany in 1913-14, and made agreements with her leaders about the reversion of the Portuguese colonies in Africa and about the building of the Baghdad railway, the situation in the Balkans remained a threat to peace. When, on 28th June 1914, the Archduke Franz Ferdinand, the Austro-Hungarian heir-apparent, was murdered by Serbian nationalists at Sarajevo in Bosnia, his country's leaders evidently welcomed the excuse this afforded for an attack on Serbia. Some weeks were taken up in preparation, and then on 23rd July an ultimatum with a 48-hour time-limit was sent to the Serbian Government. Although the Serbs gave way on nearly all points, the Austro-Hungarians took their reply as a rejection of the ultimatum and declared war on Serbia on 28th July. For this action they had already secured German approval. On the 30th Russia began to mobilise in retaliation, and on hearing of this the Germans did the same, and then sent an ultimatum to Russia, followed by a declaration of war on 1st August. Meanwhile on 31st July the French had begun to mobilise, and Germany declared war on France on 3rd August. Late on 2nd August, in preparation for an invasion of France through Belgium, Germany had sent a 12-hour ultimatum to the Belgians demanding free passage of German troops through

their territory; and early on 4th August the invasion of
Belgium began.

The course of these events seemed to people in Britain
bewilderingly rapid. Grey, who had not expected a sudden
disturbance of the peace so long after the Archduke's assassina-
tion, was very alarmed by the presentation of the Austrian
ultimatum to Serbia. He at once proposed his usual remedy
—a London conference of ambassadors. But on 27th July
Germany abruptly refused, and it soon became evident that a
European war would result. The members of the Cabinet
were by no means all convinced of the need for British intervention on the side of Russia and France; and on the 30th
Grey was obliged to inform the French ambassador that
Britain might remain neutral. He personally realised to the
full, however, the moral obligations to France that the staff
talks had imposed; and if the question of Belgium had not
arisen he might have found himself in an intolerable position
in the Cabinet—an advocate of action, disavowed by his
colleagues.

The question of Belgium, however, made all the difference.
Britain was a guarantor of Belgian neutrality under the Treaty
of 1839; and it was much to her interest to secure respect for
this. As it happened, the German military plan required an
invasion of Belgium, and no great concern was felt in Berlin
as to whether or not this would involve British intervention,
owing to the small size of the British Army. Consequently,
when on 2nd August the Germans sent their ultimatum to
Belgium, the issue facing the British Cabinet was transformed:
the Radicals were converted to the standpoint of Grey, and
only a small minority—John Burns and John Morley—
remained as advocates of neutrality.

On the afternoon of 3rd August Parliament met, and Grey
argued the case for war—not so much for France's sake,
although he stressed the moral obligation to her, as for
Belgium's. He received strong support from the Conservative
leaders, and from the Irish under John Redmond; but
Ramsay MacDonald, for the forty-strong Labour Party, dis-
sented from the general unanimity. (Next day it transpired
that the Labour Party too was willing to swing over on the
Belgian issue; and MacDonald, who with a Socialist minority

continued to oppose the war, was forced to resign his leadership.)   Sure of almost completely united national support, the
Government dispatched an ultimatum to Germany to respect
Belgian neutrality ;   the ultimatum expired without satisfaction on the night of 4th August, at 11 p.m.   At that hour
there was some cheering in Whitehall ;   but most of the
country took the declaration of war with silent surprise.   This
was no mere colonial adventure ;   and although there were
few who thought the war would last more than a few months,
it was generally accepted that Britain was facing a more
serious challenge to her power than she had had to face for a
hundred years.

★

The politics of the years immediately succeeding the South
African War had exhibited a remarkable swing against the
party in power.   The Conservative Government lost favour
rapidly—as much as anything because of the innovations of
policy which it boldly sought to impose upon a reluctant
public.   These innovations were principally the work of
Balfour, a man of intellectual power rather than political skill,
who succeeded his uncle, the great Lord Salisbury, as Prime
Minister in 1902.
It was natural that there should be a certain reaction
against the Government as disillusionment grew over the
situation in South Africa, where guerrilla warfare continued
until 1902 ;   but if this had been all, the long time which the
Government could run from the election of the new Parliament
in 1900 might well have sufficed to enable it to recover popular
favour.   Balfour disposed of this possibility by embarking on
a number of reforming measures which antagonised important
and articulate sections of the public.   The first of these was
the Education Act of 1902, which opened up valuable opportunities for the expansion of secondary education with state
assistance.   Unfortunately, the Act aroused the wrath of the
nonconformists by strengthening the position of the Church of
England schools, many of which were expecting to have to
close down through lack of funds.   Consequently, although the
Liberal leader supported the measure, a vigorous campaign
against it led by Lloyd George began to rally nonconformity

once more to the Liberal Party. A Licensing Act of 1904, which provided for the compensation of publicans who lost their licences out of a fund raised by levy on the whole trade, completed the disillusionment of the nonconformists with the Government.

But if these measures caused a rallying of nonconformist opposition against the Government, they were not as important in strengthening and heartening the Liberal Party and weakening the Conservatives as was Chamberlain's campaign for Tariff Reform and Balfour's handling of the issue. It was in May 1903 that Chamberlain, the Colonial Secretary, came out with his fiscal proposals ; and Balfour, unwilling to make up his mind at once on so important an issue, provoked the resignation from his Cabinet not only of Chamberlain but also of the keenest free trade supporters among his colleagues, including C. T. Ritchie, the Chancellor of the Exchequer. As a further mark of his indecision he replaced Ritchie by Chamberlain's son, Austen.

Joseph Chamberlain's insistence on campaigning the country on behalf of Tariff Reform only served further to strengthen the Liberal Party at the expense of the Conservatives, whose divisions on the question became more and more serious. Many industrial leaders, fearful for their exports to foreign countries, announced their opposition to Chamberlain, a tendency most marked in traditionally Conservative Lancashire. Trade-union leaders declared their hostility to any tariffs that might cause a rise in prices at the expense of working-class standards ; and the Secretary of the Labour Representation Committee, Ramsay MacDonald, entered into a secret agreement with the Liberals for mutual support in the constituencies at the forthcoming general election.

The unfortunate Government, apparently, could do nothing right. A storm suddenly arose on an issue affecting the situation in South Africa—an issue of little direct importance to the people of Britain, but one which infuriated a surprisingly large number of them. Against Chamberlain's opposition, the Cabinet had agreed to the importation into the Transvaal of considerable numbers of indentured Chinese coolies, who were to work in the mines and to live in specially segregated compounds. They were, it seemed, to work virtually as slaves, in an area which Britons had so lately fought to open up for the free immigration of their own kinsmen. ' Chinese labour ' was thus an issue which aroused strong feelings on economic, humanitarian, and patriotic grounds alike.

The Government's only major political success at this time was its Irish policy, which consisted of ' killing Home Rule by kindness ' : a generous Land Purchase Act was initiated by Wyndham, the Chief Secretary, and passed in 1903, and it had a beneficial effect on the root-cause of much of the peasant agitation. Needless to say, however, it did not win the Irish Nationalists to an alliance with the Conservative Party. Nor did the Government's last major measure, the Unemployed Workmen Act of 1905, cut much ice with labour, for its beneficial effects were very limited : it authorised the establishment of local bodies to collect information about unemployment and, if voluntary subscriptions were forthcoming, it permitted their use for the provision of work for the unemployed. After the passage of this Act, the dissensions in the Conservative Party between Tariff Reformers and Free Traders became still more acute. Early in December 1905 Balfour, realising that the Liberals were themselves still divided over some issues, decided to resign without dissolving. He thus forced the Liberal leader, Sir Henry Campbell-Bannerman, to form a government before ' going to the country ', and evidently hoped that difficulties in forming a Liberal Cabinet would serve to weaken the Liberals in the following general election.

Campbell-Bannerman, himself a Radical of a fairly moderate type, in fact had little difficulty in reconciling the various sections of his party. He gave the Liberal Imperialists many of the key offices—Asquith the Exchequer, Grey the Foreign Office, and Haldane the War Office. But he was assisted by the fact that Rosebery, who had been the leader of the Liberal Imperialists, preferred to stay out. Of the Gladstonian Radicals, Morley went to the India Office and Lloyd George to the Board of Trade ; and John Burns, the former Socialist and ' hero ' of the dock strike of 1889, but now a steady Gladstonian, became the first working man to enter the Cabinet, which he did as President of the Local Government Board.

The general election soon followed, in January 1906 ; and it resulted in an overwhelming victory for the Liberal Party, which gained 399 seats and thus held an ample margin over all other parties combined. The Unionists sank to 157, of whom two-thirds were Tariff Reformers ; the Irish Nationalists numbered 83 ; and there were 29 members of the Labour Representation Committee, who promptly constituted themselves as a new and distinct party in the House of Commons —the Labour Party. Although the election had largely been fought on Tariff Reform and ' Chinese labour ', it was significant that there was now a large body of trade-union leaders in the House, mostly in the Labour Party, as well as many social reformers in the Liberal ranks.

The first legislative work of the new Ministry was designed to reverse the innovations of the previous Government, which the electorate had now pronounced against. The recruiting of Chinese labour for South Africa was stopped, and autonomy was restored to the Boer states. A Trades Disputes Act was passed to give the unions the protection for their funds that they had lost by the Taff Vale decision of 1901. But an Education Bill designed to satisfy the nonconformists was killed by the House of Lords, in defiance of the verdict of the electorate—an action which, more than any other, caused the Liberals to set about framing ways to limit the Lords' power. Meanwhile Haldane was reorganising the Army, with some legislative help ; Lloyd George, at the Board of Trade, was making a reputation as an administrator and a conciliator of industrial disputes ; and Asquith at the Exchequer was doing his best to remove all food taxes. The only measures of social reform in the first two years of the Liberal Ministry were an Act of 1906 to permit local authorities to provide meals for necessitous school-children, and an Old Age Pensions Act of 1908 which provided 5s a week each for old people over 70, or 7s 6d for married couples. Old age pensions had been under discussion for so long that it did not seem a very revolutionary measure for the Liberals to introduce, especially as their proposals were so very limited in scope. Not yet could the Government claim to be treating social reform as a high priority.

In 1908, however, important changes took place in the

Ministry. Campbell-Bannerman died, to be succeeded by Asquith, who belonged to the former Liberal Imperialist group. To redress the balance of forces in the Cabinet he promoted Lloyd George to the Exchequer, putting a successful under-secretary, the young Winston Churchill, at the Board of Trade. This took place just at a time when the Liberals seemed to be losing support in the country : the by-elections showed a trend to the Tariff Reformers on the one hand and to Socialism on the other. Lloyd George, faced with the need for finding more money for naval rearmament in the 1909 fiscal year, determined to use the budget as a weapon of social change, raising the necessary extra revenue almost exclusively from the wealthy. If the Lords should attempt to interfere with his proposals, in Lloyd George's view it would be so much the better. He realised that a struggle on the constitutional issue would do the Liberals no harm and might considerably improve their electoral prospects.

The budget of 1909 introduced a number of novelties : taxes on petrol and motor licences, to pay for road improve- ments ; reductions in income-tax rates for parents of young children ; a new super-tax ; and—most remarkable of all— a duty of 20 per cent on ' the unearned increment of land value ', to be paid whenever land changed hands. It was this last proposal which particularly incensed the Lords, many of whom were substantial landowners. A furious controversy developed, much to Lloyd George's delight ; and soon the Conservative leadership had committed itself to the rejection of the budget in the Lords—an action of doubtful consti- tutional validity, and one which inevitably precipitated a general election. This took place in January 1910.

The results of the election were such as to provide the Liberals, and Lloyd George in particular, with a sense of satisfaction at the success of their tactics. They certainly lost a good many seats, but nothing like as many as they would have lost had they fought on any other issue. They returned with 275 members, against the Unionists' 273 ; but they had as allies 40 members of the Labour Party and 82 Irish Nationalists. The Lords now permitted the passage of the budget ; but the Ministry was determined to settle the constitutional issue for the future, and so it introduced a

Parliament Bill to allow the enactment of legislation which had been approved in three successive sessions of the Lower House, whether the Lords approved it or not. Now the acute constitutional issue arose : would the King authorise the creation of a large number of peers by the Ministry if the Lords refused to acquiesce in the diminution of their own powers ? The Conservatives thought that he should not ; the Liberals thought that he should. It was an issue that threatened to bring the Crown into the very centre of the political controversy.

Edward VII's handling of this difficult situation was skilful. Before the election he had told Asquith in confidence that he would create the necessary peers only after a second general election on the issue of the Parliament Bill. In the middle of the crisis, however, he died suddenly, and in the hush of party strife that this caused, his son, George V, endeavoured to secure a compromise between the parties. Although Lloyd George made some interesting proposals for a Coalition Government, which attracted some at least of the Conservative leaders, the negotiations fell through, and the King reaffirmed his father's attitude to the Parliament Bill. A second general election was therefore held in December 1910, and the results were very similar indeed to those of the previous January : the Liberal and Labour Parties combined still had a majority of 42 over the Conservatives. Early in 1911, under the threat of the creation of large numbers of Liberal peers, the Lords gave way and passed the Parliament Bill. By its provisions the veto power of the Lords was reduced to a power of delaying legislation for two years ; and as a compensation for this, the maximum length of time between general elections for the Lower House was reduced from seven years to five. The balance of the constitution had been altered, but it had been altered only as much as was absolutely necessary for the ending of the legislative deadlock.

The year 1911 was a year not only of constitutional change but also of growing labour unrest and international crisis. The Osborne judgment of 1909 had made it illegal for trade unions to impose a compulsory levy on their members for the purposes of parliamentary representation, and this placed the Labour Members who depended on union money for their salaries, in an acutely embarrassing position. It also encouraged the unions themselves, or at least the rank-and-file unionists, to veer towards policies of 'direct action' and syndicalism—using strikes for political as much as for purely industrial purposes. The Agadir crisis, already discussed, threatened international war and led to the acceleration of plans to deal with such an emergency. The Commons had to play its part in dealing with these new difficulties : to relieve the Labour Members it was decided to inaugurate the state payment of M.P.s ; and to deal with the possibility of military espionage in Britain an Official Secrets Act was passed.

But the most important measure of the year, after the Parliament Act, was a measure of social legislation—the National Insurance Act introduced by Lloyd George and Winston Churchill. The Act, partly modelled on the system in existence in Germany, was primarily a contributory scheme to insure the working population against sickness ; but coupled with it was a somewhat less comprehensive scheme for insurance against unemployment. The Friendly Societies which had long been in existence were permitted to become 'approved societies' for the purposes of the administration of the Act. But the doctors and many of the employers disliked what they regarded as an element of regimentation in the operation of the measure, and it was hotly opposed, though not to the extent of a Lords' rejection.

In 1912 the Government passed to the highly controversial issue of Irish Home Rule—an issue that underlay much of the bitterness of the Parliament Bill struggle. The Home Rule Bill that the Ministry proposed provided for an Irish Parliament at Dublin and a limited Irish representation at Westminster. The main disadvantage of the Bill was its failure to cater for the special problem posed by the Ulster minority, whose economic, social, and religious life was so different from that of the rest of the Irish people, and whose capital, Belfast, was growing rapidly and challenging the primacy of Dublin. The Conservative Party, which had replaced Balfour as its leader with the more combative Bonar Law (himself a Presbyterian of Ulster origin), was now determined to make the most of the Ulster problem in order to defeat the Bill. The Liberals on the other hand were so dependent on the parliamentary support of the Irish Nationalists under John Redmond that they could not afford to make any changes in the Bill for Ulster's sake. The result was that while the Bill steadily passed through the various stages of its transition to the statute book that were required by the Parliament Act— it finally became law after the necessary period of delay in 1914—the situation in Ireland steadily deteriorated and approached the brink of civil war. On the one hand, Bonar Law gave *carte blanche* to the Ulstermen, under their leader Sir Edward Carson, to proceed to any degree of revolt if necessary, and Carson's Ulster Volunteers soon became a substantial force. On the other hand, the Irish Nationalists apparently only had to stand firm at Westminster for their aims to be realised ; but behind their backs in Ireland a younger generation was building up the more extreme ' Sinn Fein ' movement, which set about recruiting a force to counter the Ulstermen—the Irish Volunteers. In March 1914 some unfortunate blunders in the military command led to the resignation of fifty-eight army officers stationed in Ireland, who were in a unit expected to have to undertake the ' coercion ' of Ulster. This was the so-called ' Curragh Mutiny '. The whole question remained quite unresolved when—mercifully, in the short run, for Ireland—war broke out on the Continent in August 1914.

The Liberal Government must share with the Opposition the responsibility for the drift towards civil war on the Irish issue. But its difficulties were by no means limited to this issue ; for as the parliamentary struggle became steadily more and more bitter, it is not surprising that popular movements for other objects, when thwarted by parliamentary opposition, moved rapidly towards unconstitutional action. The strikes of 1911 and the syndicalist movement have already been mentioned ; they constantly taxed the capacity of ministers to find peaceful solutions, and involved the use of troops on several occasions, notably on Merseyside in 1911 and in South Wales in 1912. They culminated in 1913 in the permanent threat of a ' general strike '—the ' Triple Alliance ' of the railway men, transport workers, and miners, which was not invoked until after the war. More immediately sensational was the ' Suffragette ' campaign, the work of the militant wing of the women's suffrage movement. This campaign, under the leadership of the redoubtable Mrs Emmeline Pankhurst and her daughter Christabel, greatly embarrassed members of all parties, and ministers most of all. In 1910–11 various attempts were made to pass a Bill to suit the movement, but the violent campaign alienated many M.P.s and made them less sympathetic. Failing to win the support of Parliament, the Suffragettes began a campaign of arson, directed by Christabel Pankhurst from Paris. The perpetrators of the outrages, if caught and imprisoned, went on hunger strike, and forcible feeding was then introduced by the Government. In 1913 the danger of a prisoner dying on hunger strike was reduced by the Government's ' Cat and Mouse ' Act, which allowed for the early release of those in poor health, and for the resumption of their sentence when they recovered. Such were the extremes of violence which marked the last years of peacetime Liberal government—years which paradoxically the people of Britain were soon to look back to as an age of care-free tranquillity.

★

Although about two and a half million people emigrated from Britain in these years—a total by no means balanced by a small trickle of Eastern European immigrants escaping from the pogroms of Czarism—the population of Great Britain, though not of Ireland, continued to rise steadily. By 1911 it amounted to 40·8 million, an increase of almost four million in ten years. The birth-rate was steadily declining, from 28·2 per thousand in 1900 to 23·9 in 1913 ; but the decline in the death-rate from 18·4 to 14·2 in the same period compensated for this. As the principal improvement was a reduction of infantile mortality—caused by improved medical practice and by the influence of ' health visitors ' employed by municipal authorities—the age composition of the population cannot have changed very much in the period, although a certain tendency for the proportion of old people to rise was already in existence.

We have seen that many of the country's industries changed comparatively little in this period. There was, however, a great improvement in domestic transport facilities. Electric trams were introduced in many large towns, replacing the much slower horse-drawn trams. Many of the tram companies were run by the local corporations, for ' municipal socialism ' was making more progress than ever. In London, however, the great advances of the period were made by privately owned underground railway and motor-bus companies. Everywhere the effect was the same : people found that they could live farther from their work. There was as a result a great deal of house-building on the outskirts of London and other cities and towns. These new suburbs often consisted of very cheap and small red-brick houses, catering for a new lower middle class.

The private motor car, however, was not yet generally available. It was too expensive ; and even the wealthy used their cars much more for recreation than for business purposes. Raising clouds of dust as they went by, the cars were an object of resentment for poorer people, at least until Lloyd George's budget of 1909 inaugurated a road fund which was used to pay for tarring the surfaces. Meanwhile air travel was making its first experimental progress ; it was an American invention developed first in Europe by Frenchmen. In 1909 the first crossing of the Channel by air was effected by the French aviator Blériot. Within another four years the feat had been performed by several Britons including, significantly, a woman. But aviation remained in a purely experimental stage.

Other inventions also made their mark, some of them more immediately practical. The gramophone could be used for the recording of speeches or of music, though there was still a good deal of hiss from the needle. Typewriters were widely used, and the female typist-secretary was beginning to make an appearance. Wireless telegraphy, invented by the Italian Marconi, owed much to development in Britain, and soon came into use for shipping : in 1910 an escaping criminal, Dr Crippen, was arrested on board ship as a result of its use. The loss, with two-thirds of her passengers and crew, of the supposedly unsinkable White Star liner *Titanic* on her maiden voyage to New York, as a result of hitting an iceberg, showed that plenty of natural hazards still remained to be conquered ; but without the use of wireless it is probable that there would have been no survivors.

Since real wages made little progress in this period, there could not be much improvement in the condition of the working people, other than that directly due to medical advances. Poverty was still the major problem; and Rowntree, investigating social conditions at York, found that 27·8 per cent of the total population—or 43·4 per cent of the wage-earning class—were below the income level necessary to satisfy minimum household needs. It was inferred from this that probably 30 per cent of the total British population was below the Rowntree standard : a guess, but one that must have been somewhere near the truth. Much was done by legislation to improve conditions for specially depressed groups : Churchill's Trade Boards Act of 1909 was in response to an agitation against conditions in the so-called ' sweated ' industries, and resulted in considerable advances. The establishment of labour exchanges in the same year on the recommendation of W. H. Beveridge helped to reduce the destitution caused by casual employment. The National Insurance Act was also a considerable step forward, although its arrangements for dealing with unemployment by no means covered the whole population. Old age pensions and the beginnings of municipal feeding of school children also made some contribution. But all these measures were piecemeal and covered no very large proportion of the privations of the poor. In London men were still sleeping out on the Embankment in large numbers, queuing up at the soup-kitchens, running after cabs in order to earn a tip for opening the door. A Royal Commission on the Poor Law which reported in 1909 produced a Majority and a Minority Report, the latter being the work of the Fabian Socialist, Mrs Beatrice Webb : she advocated the break-up of the old Poor Law system, with its harsh conditions designed to discourage idleness, and the redistribution of its work among other departments responsible for social welfare. But the Local Government Board under John Burns, himself of working-class background, was stubbornly conservative, and very little was done.

All the same it was a novelty that so much social legislation was placed on the statute book, and that the educated population was so keenly interested in social problems, which were expounded to them by various authors in ever-growing statistical detail. This was partly due to the growth of the professional classes, many of whom were directly concerned with these things. It was also rendered possible by the popular loss of interest in the problems of imperialism after the South African War. Although, as we have seen, the issues that bulked large in the 1906 election were not primarily social issues, there were many social reformers who then secured election to Parliament, and their influence was important. So too was that of the Labour Party, which, if not always capable of initiating the complex legislation that was required, was for the most part very anxious to support it. The doctrine of Socialism made considerable progress, both among the working class, who in increasing numbers joined the I.L.P. (which was affiliated to the Labour Party) or the smaller Socialist bodies—the S.D.F., the Clarion Fellowship, and so on ; and also among some of the middle class who responded to the more intellectual appeal of the Fabians. The most sensational political victory for Socialism in the period was at a 1907 by-election in the Yorkshire industrial constituency of Colne Valley, where Victor Grayson, standing as a Socialist without Labour Party support, won a three-cornered fight for a formerly Liberal seat. This may have had some influence in persuading the Liberals to press forward with social reform in later years.

As time went on, however, the militancy of the working class turned more and more into purely industrial channels. This may be illustrated by the story of the workers' educational movement, which developed in these years. In 1899 a residential workers' college, Ruskin Hall, was established at Oxford, and it had affiliated groups throughout the country. There was also a Workers' Educational Association founded in 1903. In 1909, however, some of the workers already resident at Oxford demanded a more ' Marxist ' educational curriculum, and seceded to form a body of their own—the Labour College. This body, which secured financial support from the miners and railwaymen in particular, grew rapidly in importance and went into competition with the Workers' Educational Association. It encouraged syndicalist ideas and contributed much to the militancy of the labour movement after 1910, and to the tendency towards amalgamation among existing unions in the same industry.   Its influence may be seen in the creation of the National Union of Railwaymen, out of three existing unions, in 1913 and in the formation of the ' Triple Alliance ' already mentioned.   Trade-union membership in total advanced from less than two million in 1901 to over four million in 1914 ;   and by the Trade Union Act of 1913 the unions recovered the right to make contributions for political purposes—albeit from a special fund, from which union members would have the opportunity of ' contracting out '.

Meanwhile the opportunities of the state educational system had been substantially expanded by the unpopular Education Act of 1902.   The functions of the democratic, but often inefficient, School Boards were taken over by the County and County Borough Councils ;   and the task of building up a state secondary school system was slowly begun.   By 1914 there were about 200,000 children in grant-aided secondary schools —not a large proportion of the total population, but at least a beginning.   Few of them could find their way to Oxford or Cambridge ;   but now the university colleges in the provinces —Liverpool, Manchester, Leeds, Sheffield, Bristol—secured full autonomy, and London University was expanding considerably.   The study of modern subjects, including economics and various branches of science, made great progress, even at the older universities.   At Cambridge, indeed, revolutionary work on the structure of the atom was being conducted by J. J. Thomson.   The publication of books seems to have responded readily to these educational advances :   the annual number of new titles rose from about 5,000 in 1900 to twice as many in 1913 ;   and the proportion of the total which were on technical subjects increased.

The growth in the number of books published was some compensation for the decline of the better class of independent newspapers.   In this period the Harmsworth type of journalism flourished, and overtook many of the best provincial papers. The three leaders of the growing commercial popular press were Harmsworth himself, Pearson, and Hulton ;   and Harmsworth, whose *Daily Mail* was the most successful of all the dailies, completed his triumph in 1908 by buying *The Times*. This gave him enormous power for good and evil in influencing all classes of the community.

The arts—most of them being as always the preserve of
cultural minorities—responded to the serious tone of the
educated public.   It was the theatre that made the most
remarkable progress in this period ; and the leading playwrights were for the most part social moralists, anxious to
expound and to argue.   The most successful was, of course,
Bernard Shaw, whose brilliant wit delighted, if it did not
always convince, his audiences.   Next to him came Galsworthy, also a social critic, but simpler and less paradoxical
in his moralising.   Barrie, more purely imaginative than either
of the other two, was less typical of the age.   Theatrical
production improved very much at the same time, the producer taking the place of the actor-manager ;   Harley
Granville-Barker was a pioneer of this change, and he succeeded in revolutionising Shakespearean production, treating
the original text with unwonted respect.   Only at the end of
the period did the stage begin to experience for the first time
the rivalry of the moving picture—which for the most part
still took the form of a variety show rather than a continuous
drama.

Almost equally successful with the theatre in this period
was the novel ; and here the effects of popular education
were marked.   Social criticism was prominent in the work of
H. G. Wells and Galsworthy in particular ; and Wells was a
pioneer in the field of science fiction—an indication of the
progress of scientific knowledge.   Henry James and George
Moore who represented a more intimate and personal type of
literature were less widely read.   A cool Cambridge rational-
ism was reflected in the novels of E. M. Forster, and also in
the philosophy of G. E. Moore and Bertrand Russell.   Poetry
was much neglected ; and the most popular type was not
lyric poetry but narrative—notably that of John Masefield.
The fantasy of G. K. Chesterton and the satire of Hilaire
Belloc linked Anglo-Catholicism and Roman Catholicism
respectively to a strong social criticism akin to that of the
syndicalists.   Painting rather slavishly followed the French lead
in Impressionism and Post-impressionism.   Musical composition, with Elgar and Vaughan Williams, reached unaccustomed
heights, and much work was done in collecting the fast-
disappearing English folk-songs.   Architecture and craftsman-

ship, both still feeling the influence of William Morris, were moving away from traditional conceptions; and town-planning, under the patronage of rich business men such as Lever and Cadbury, began to be practised again, as at Port Sunlight and Bournville.

The growing extent of the towns and—by and large—their continued squalor encouraged people to escape into the countryside on Sundays or holidays or on the Saturday half-holiday which was now becoming normal for the factory or office worker. Cycling continued to grow in popularity, and cycling clubs expanded, including the Clarion clubs run by Blatchford's paper. The idea of 'scouting' pioneered by Blatchford was now taken up in earnest in more 'respectable' quarters : General Baden-Powell, the defender of Mafeking, initiated the Boy Scout movement with his book *Scouting for Boys* (1906), which emphasised the importance of training for the outdoor life ; and soon Boy Scouts and Girl Guides were to be seen about the countryside, learning how to cook open-air meals and live in tented camps. At a time when so many of the population were unfit, as was shown by the medical testing of recruits both in the South African War and in the World War fifteen years later, this movement could not be other than extremely beneficial.

All these characteristics of the period may seem to belie the concept of Edwardian grandeur which has become current in recent years—the picture of aristocratic society enjoying the last flowering of elegance and grace before the twentieth-century deluge of war, state control, and equalitarianism. That such a society did exist at the top of the social pyramid cannot be denied ; and King Edward himself, by his frank enjoyment of the pleasures that wealth could bring, gave it a tone of frivolity which it had not had in his mother's reign. In 1908 he even made Asquith kiss hands as Prime Minister in a hotel room at Biarritz. Those who had money, whether inherited or not, lost little of it in taxation, even after Lloyd George had done his worst ; and the greater freedom of movement which technology permitted, and the change in manners which this encouraged, made the spending of the rich more conspicuous than before.

All the same, even this class was being profoundly affected

by the triumph of the urban middle class. The young aristocrat was now educated at a ' public ' school instead of by
private tutors ; he played organised games there, even if he
also joined in the recreations of the wealthy ; and he normally
entered upon some profession or business, instead of simply
living the life of a gentleman of leisure. As for the young
women, they too went to school and often to college, and
many of them embarrassed their families by lending encouragement to the Suffragette campaign. Thus, already before 1914,
things were not what they had been ' in the good old days '.

The alterations in costume which took place in the period
illustrate these social changes. Men wore frock coats only for
the most formal occasions ; lounge coats became increasingly
popular, and after about 1910 the dinner jacket came in
instead of tails for respectable evening wear. Home-spun
tweeds were now quite suitable for informal occasions.
Women's clothes became lighter and less tightly corseted ;
although hair styles and hats were both ungainly, skirts were
not so long as before and sometimes they exposed part of the
leg above the ankle. All this indicated a desire for dress
which would permit greater freedom of activity on the part of
the wearer. There was also a great development of ready-
made clothes, which led to an increased uniformity of appearance—an important change in the direction of the readier
mingling of people of all classes. In the character of these
changes there was, as we shall see in later chapters, a certain
inherent continuity.

4 The First World War, 1914-18

BRITAIN entered the war in a very fair state of preparation —at least, for a country which refused to maintain a large standing army. The Navy, which was already mobilised, was ready for its immediate tasks, and the so-called Grand Fleet under Admiral Sir John Jellicoe was at once constituted and established at Scapa to keep watch for any attempt at action by the German High Seas Fleet. The expeditionary force, at a strength of some 90,000, was sent to France under the command of General Sir John French, of Boer War fame; composed of skilled riflemen, it proved its worth in the fighting retreat of the French armies in front of Paris in late August and early September. After rearguard actions at Mons and Le Cateau, it thrust back at a gap in the enemy lines on the Marne, and thus helped to check the German advance and stabilise the line, which after the fall of Antwerp in October ran from the Channel ports to the French fortresses of the Alsace-Lorraine front, with a big salient in the direction of Paris. But after further heavy fighting at Ypres in October and November there was little left of the original British expeditionary force : it could hold only 21 miles of line as against 430 held by the French. The 'contemptible' little British army, as the Kaiser was reported to have termed it, had proved its worth, but it could not continue to play a significant role without heavy reinforcement.

The hopes of the Western Allies at first turned to the eastern front, where the 'Russian steam-roller', descending on a thinly defended German frontier, was expected to advance with speed. But the Russian armies in the north had already been sent into reverse after a crushing defeat at the Battle of Tannenberg (28th August) ; and although an Austrian offensive against Poland failed with even heavier loss, German support enabled the eastern front to be stabilised. Further heavy fighting in November did not result in any important change before the onset of winter. The British Navy was meanwhile hunting down and destroying the few units of the German fleet that were on foreign stations ; a minor German success at the Battle of Coronel off the Chilean coast was speedily avenged with the aid of reinforcements from the Grand Fleet at the Battle of the Falkland Isles. All save one of the German warships ' at large ' had been eliminated by the end of 1914 ; but the main German fleet for the time being preferred not to venture a decisive combat. Various minor operations to occupy the German colonies were under way ; but the only means of breaking the apparent deadlock in Europe seemed to be provided by the entry of Turkey into the war on the side of Germany and Austria in October.

Meanwhile new British armies were being rapidly recruited and trained. The first of the wartime volunteers, together with the existing Territorial force of about 250,000 and contingents from the Dominions, were available for service early in 1915. After the receipt of an appeal from Russia for assistance against Turkey, it was decided to commit a small proportion of them to a landing at the Dardanelles. Unfortunately, however, this operation began in February with a purely naval bombardment, followed by an attempt on the part of the fleet to force the narrows into the Black Sea. This attack, which failed owing to the presence of mines, gave the Turks time to strengthen their defences with German assistance before the landing of troops took place at Gallipoli in April. Lacking the element of surprise, the landing force under General Sir Ian Hamilton was not strong enough to win its objectives, and after heavy casualties it held little more than its beach positions. A further landing effected in August at Suvla Bay also failed to achieve a decision. When the weather deteriorated in the autumn an evacuation became imperative, and this was successfully undertaken in December 1915 and January 1916—the one part of a very costly campaign that was conducted with real skill.

Meanwhile the western front had settled down to an affair of trenches and barbed wire, and in the technical conditions of the time defensive operations obtained a considerable

FIRST WORLD WAR
1914–1918
- - - - Front line at end of 1914
———— Front line on 11th Nov. 1918

0 10 20 30 40 50 60 70 MILES

advantage. The arts of camouflage and deception were rudi-
mentary, and while both sides had a few aircraft for reconnais-
sance, neither could achieve the type of air superiority which
could prevent enemy observation. Heavy artillery bombardment could do something to prepare for an offensive, but it
could not neutralise a well-entrenched and determined defence,
which with a few machine-guns could take a heavy toll of
advancing infantry. But the commanders on either side, and
not least the British, were slow to appreciate these facts. The
new British army lost heavily in offensives at Neuve-Chapelle
in March and at Festubert in May 1915, and Sir John French's
insistence for prestige purposes on holding an exposed salient
at Ypres caused a further heavy drain of casualties. At this

time, however, reinforcements were more than making up for
losses, and the British army in France grew to a total of
twenty-one divisions in July. This increase in strength, coupled
with the heavy commitments of the Germans on the Russian
fronts, encouraged the Western Allies to launch a fresh
offensive in September 1915. The Battle of Loos, as the
struggle in the British sector was called, was virtually a defeat,
partly at least owing to Sir John French's failure to throw in
his reserves at the decisive moment. Shortly afterwards he
was replaced by a corps commander, Sir Douglas Haig. In
the east the Russians had by this time been forced to evacuate
Poland and were standing entirely on the defensive ; and
Bulgaria was encouraged to enter the war on the German side
and to join in an offensive against Serbia, which resulted in
the entire occupation of that unhappy country. It was no
great consolation that Italy had entered the war on the Allied
side (May 1915), for the Italian forces could do little more
than hold their own against the Austrians.

The beginning of 1916 thus found three main fronts of war
in existence—the eastern (Russia), the western (Britain and
France), and the southern (Italy). By comparison with these
the ' sideshows '—such as the Anglo-French position at Salonika
in Greece and the British operations against Turkey in Meso-
potamia—were of little importance. The war had already
proved very costly to the French, who had had two million
casualties ; and the British, though still increasing the size of
their armies, had lost half a million, including the bulk of the
peacetime forces. The German command, with the advantage of the inner lines of communication, therefore determined
to attack again in the west and in February launched a heavy
attack against the French fortress of Verdun. The assault,
which made very slow progress, was continued all through the
spring and was broken off only in July, with Verdun still in
French hands. By this time the British armies had built up
considerably, and they were naturally expected to relieve the
pressure on their allies by taking the offensive.

There ensued what became known as the Battle of the
Somme. Elaborate preparations for the offensive took place,
but they were very obvious to the enemy. There was an
artillery bombardment of the German positions, but this was

inadequate, for the British forces were seriously short of artillery. After this the infantry were sent forward in broad daylight, and weighed down with 66 lb. of equipment each. According to the Official History this weight ' made it difficult to get out of a trench, impossible to move much quicker than a slow walk, or to rise and lie down quickly '. On the first day alone (1st July) the army lost 60,000 men ; yet the attacks were renewed until October, and when they were done there was little to show for the vast effort. At a total cost of 420,000 British casualties, an advance of seven miles was made on a thirty-mile front, with no clear strategic advantage as a result. The German casualties, which were rather more than two to every three of the Allies', were inflated by the insistence of the German command on the recapture of all lost ground. One feature of the battle was the use of tanks, a British invention ; but there were too few of them to make much difference to the outcome.

The pattern of developments on the eastern front in 1916 was not dissimilar from that of 1915 : Russian successes against Austrian troops were followed by decisive German intervention to restore the situation. This time the initial Russian successes brought the Rumanians into the war on the Allied side, but it did not take long for the Germans to invade and occupy most of their country. At sea the war was largely developing into a German submarine offensive against Allied and neutral shipping. But in May 1916 a major fleet action was fought between the British and German navies in the North Sea. Known in Britain as the Battle of Jutland, it ended indecisively, with the German fleet retiring hastily to port after having inflicted much heavier casualties than it received. The British lost 115,025 warship tons and 6,945 men ; the Germans lost 61,180 warship tons and 3,058 men. The German ships, ton for ton, were stronger and more heavily armed ; their armour-piercing shells were better, their range-finding and fire-direction more efficient. All the same, the German fleet was no match for the *Queen Elizabeth* type of battleship ; and its strength steadily deteriorated thereafter as its best officers and men were diverted to submarine warfare.

The German submarine threat had not been particularly serious in the first two years of the war, for there were at first few U-boats available. Moreover the British barrier of nets and mines across the Straits of Dover was a formidable obstacle, and the northern route was long and difficult. It was not at first customary for liners or merchant ships to be sunk without warning, but the practice gradually grew more frequent : it had considerable advantages in enabling the U-boat to escape detection and destruction. Unfortunately for the Germans, this development was strongly opposed by the neutral powers, and especially by the United States, which was supplying the Allies with many of the goods and materials of war. The sinking in May 1915 of the Cunard liner *Lusitania*, with the loss of 100 American lives, was followed by vigorous diplomatic activity, and although the United States did not intervene with armed force the Germans were obliged to promise not to sink merchant ships without warning.

By the end of 1916 the German morale had been sapped by the continuous struggle on so many war fronts for over two years. The naval blockade by the Allies was reducing living standards and threatening to cause starvation to the population. The German command was therefore inclined to desperate measures in order to secure an early decision of the war. Prominent among these was the abandonment of attempts to placate the neutrals, and the beginning of unrestricted submarine warfare in February 1917. This was in the belief that it was more important to strike immediate blows at Britain than to keep America out of the war. Already from October 1916 the monthly toll of Allied shipping had been over 300,000 tons ; by April 1917 it rose to 875,000. But in April the United States entered the war ; and thereafter the position gradually improved, partly as a result of American and Japanese naval assistance, partly by the introduction of the convoy system, and partly by the construction of further elaborate mine barriers across the North Sea and elsewhere.

Also early in 1917 the German command decided to forestall further offensives on the western front by a retreat to a carefully prepared defensive line, known to the Germans as the Siegfried Line, but called by the Allies the Hindenburg Line. It lay some twenty-five miles behind the existing front. This decision was of great value to the German army, for when General Nivelle, the new French commander, organised

Plate 5 ADVENT OF THE MOTOR CAR. Spectators arriving for the Derby, 1911.

Plate 6 THE WAR IN FLANDERS. (*Above*) British infantry filing past bomb craters.
(*Below*) A wrecked British tank on the battlefield.

a joint attack by British and French troops in April, his plans were soon frustrated by the new defence in depth. Although the British won Vimy Ridge, a useful strategic point in front of Arras, the failure of the French led to mutinies in the French Army and the replacement of Nivelle by Pétain, the defender of Verdun. And Pétain, in view of the state of the Army, decided to stay on the defensive until ' the Americans and the tanks ' should be available in large numbers. Haig, left to himself, then launched the long and bitter hundred-day offensive of Passchendaele (July–November)—an offensive in Flanders designed to reach the Channel ports, but in fact quickly bogged down in an agony of mud and rain with a loss of 300,000 men to the British Army.

Meanwhile the collapse of the Russians, after the March revolution which overthrew the Czar, placed the Allies in great immediate danger. The last Russian assaults took place on the Galician front in July ; they were soon broken, and the Russian forces thereupon disintegrated. The Austrians were able to divert many of their troops to the Isonzo front against Italy, where they made a rapid advance, forcing the Italians back to the line of the Piave, only fifteen miles in front of Venice. On this line the Italians rallied, and had already stabilised the position when French and British reinforcements from the western front came to their aid. The loss of forces from the western front had its effect : it prevented the British army from exploiting a victory at Cambrai in November, which had been won by the fresh use of tanks, now available in larger numbers. The Battle of Cambrai in fact ended with a counter-offensive that suggested that the initiative was passing back to German hands.

It was obvious early in 1918 that the Allies had but to hold the western front in order to win the war, for the American contribution in men and materials alike would be enormous if it had time to develop. The Germans on the other hand, with the aid of reinforcements from the eastern front, were impelled to attack in order to seek a decision before it was too late. The British Army in March 1918 was not as large as a year earlier, owing to the heavy losses of 1917 and the commitments in Italy and elsewhere. Consequently the German offensive of March and April found the British front thinly held. The attack threw General Gough's Fifth Army into retreat across the Somme and almost into complete dissolution. The crisis led for the first time to a unity of the French and British commands : Haig accepted Foch as Commander-in-Chief over himself and Pétain. A further offensive against the First Army in Flanders produced the pitch of extremity that occasioned Haig's famous General Order of the Day :

There is no other course open to us but to fight it out ! Every position must be held to the last man : there must be no retirement. With our backs to the wall and believing in the justice of our cause, each one of us must fight to the end.

Under this inspiration the defence held on, and the attack weakened, only to be resumed on the French front in May. The Germans took Soissons and were within thirty-seven miles of Paris ; but again they were held, and this time American troops, in action for the first time in considerable numbers, played a part in the battle. A further German assault on the French front in July led to a penetration over the Marne, but again it came to a standstill. Thereafter the initiative passed to the Allies.

It was to Haig's credit that he at once realised how far the German strength had been weakened by their costly offensive. In August he set on foot a series of skilful attacks on weak sections of the enemy front, which rapidly led to a turning of the main fortifications. From September onwards it was clear that the German army was on the verge of defeat. That month saw a successful American operation on another western sector ; the collapse of Bulgaria, which had lost its stiffening of German troops ; and the opening of a new full-scale offensive under Foch's direction. Foch sought to combine two gigantic pincer-jaws—a Franco-American attack between Rheims and Verdun and a British attack in Flanders, aimed at Lille. The offensive had hardly begun when Ludendorff, the German commander, demanded the formation of a new German government which would undertake peace negotiations. The blockade had been taking its toll : short of fuel and food, the German people readily succumbed to illness, and their morale was low. On 5th October Prince Max of Baden, who formed the new government, informed President Wilson of America that he was willing to treat for peace. Wilson demanded a responsible government instead of ' military masters and monarchical autocrats '. On 29th October a mutiny broke out among the seamen of the High Seas Fleet when they were ordered to sea ; on the 31st Turkey surrendered after heavy defeats in Palestine at the hands of Allenby, the British commander. On 4th November Austria capitulated, her armies in Italy having been routed at the Battle of Vittorio Veneto. In the face of growing revolution at home the Kaiser abdicated on 9th November ; and the armistice was signed on the morning of the 11th. Its terms indicated that in fact it was a capitulation : it involved the immediate evacuation of occupied territory and also of the left bank of the Rhine, as well as bridgeheads across the river ; and the fleet was to be surrendered.

The cost of the war to Britain in casualties was three-quarters of a million killed and almost one and three-quarter million wounded. Another two hundred thousand men from the Empire were killed, and twice as many wounded. The total military enlistments for Britain were over six million ; for the Empire, altogether about nine and a half million. The figures themselves convey something of the enormous effort and sacrifice involved, the political background to which we must now examine.

★

The political complexion of the Government changed little under the first impact of war. Lord Kitchener was brought in to give the benefit of his great military experience to the post of Secretary for War ; with Asquith himself and Churchill, who remained as First Lord of the Admiralty, he directed the war effort, and personally supervised the strategy of the army. Unlike Sir John French, Kitchener believed that the war would last a long time, and he at once set about recruiting a new volunteer army of half a million men to reinforce the Regulars and the Territorials.

The other political parties readily accepted this initiative. The Conservatives, the Labour Party, and even the Irish agreed to an electoral truce, and all of them collaborated in supporting the recruiting campaign. The Labour Party had decided on this course by majority vote, for Ramsay Mac-Donald and Keir Hardie, with several other I.L.P. members, were in opposition. The Irish under Redmond were induced to support the war partly by loyalty to the Liberal Government, partly by their sympathy for the cause of Belgium, a small nation attacked by a large one. The Conservatives, who were wholehearted supporters of the war, were discouraged from factious opposition by the presence in the Government of Kitchener, who was known to have Conservative sympathies. One of the Conservative leaders, F. E. Smith, was put in charge of an official Press Bureau, which set in motion a somewhat irregular censorship of news. Other Conservative leaders were taken into consultation by the Government, and gave ready co-operation. The leaders of all the parties addressed recruiting meetings throughout the country ; Lloyd George spoke eloquently of the ' glittering peaks of sacrifice ', and soon introduced a special war budget which doubled the income tax—from 9d in the pound to 1s 6d.

It was not until May 1915 that serious criticism of the existing Government began to develop. In that month concern about the shell shortage on the western front received publicity in *The Times,* and at the same time Lord Fisher, the aged but highly respected First Sea Lord, resigned because of his doubts about the value of the Dardanelles campaign. The Conservatives took the opportunity to demand the exclusion from key posts of both Haldane and Churchill, the former because of a supposed sympathy with Germany, the latter because of his sponsorship of the attack on the Dardanelles. In the controversy between ' Westerners ' and ' Easterners '— that is, between those who were for concentrating effort on the western front and those who favoured opening fresh fronts elsewhere—the Conservatives tended to the ' Westerner ' standpoint, which they shared with most military leaders, while Churchill was the keenest of the ' Easterners '. Asquith gave way to the Conservative pressure and decided to construct a Coalition Cabinet. He replaced Churchill at the Admiralty by Balfour, and persuaded Bonar Law to accept the now subordinate office of Colonial Secretary. Although Kitchener remained at the War Office, a separate Ministry of Munitions was created and placed under the vigorous direction of Lloyd George, who handed the Exchequer over to another Liberal, McKenna. The Irish decided not to take office, but Arthur Henderson, the leader of the Labour Party, was induced to accept the somewhat unsuitable position of President of the Board of Education.

Unfortunately the progress of the war in 1915 brought fresh setbacks on the western front, and these led not only to the replacement of French by Haig but also to a continued diminution of the prestige of Lord Kitchener. His position was weakened by the appointment of Sir William Robertson as Chief of the Imperial General Staff, with access to the Cabinet. Soon discussion began to centre on the question of whether military conscription should be introduced. The Labour Party and the bulk of the Liberals—but not Lloyd George—opposed its introduction, and so did Kitchener, proud as he was of his own success in securing voluntary recruits. But it became clear towards the end of 1915 that the flow of voluntary recruits was inadequate, and it seemed unjust that married men of all ages should be serving—and uneconomical that their families should be receiving subsistence allowances —while many unmarried men had refused to come forward. Lord Derby, who became Director of Recruiting in October 1915, initiated the ' Derby scheme ' as a last effort to avoid compulsion : men were invited to register, but guarantees were given that the married men would not be called up until the unmarried men had been absorbed. The scheme failed to produce the necessary recruits, and in January 1916 the Government adopted the principle of compulsion. The decision led to the resignation of only one prominent Liberal, Sir John Simon, and was accepted with little protest by the Labour Party and the trade unions.

A few months later, at Easter, an unpleasant contrast to the prevailing national unity was provided by an insurrection which broke out in Dublin. With the aid of smuggled German arms a number of extreme nationalists attempted to seize control of the city, but were defeated after a week's fierce fighting. The ringleaders were then executed in cold blood— a savage act that gave considerable encouragement to the further growth of extreme nationalism. Attempts to secure agreed changes in the existing Home Rule measure—which had only been held in abeyance by the war—were frustrated by Conservative hostility.

In June 1916 Kitchener was drowned at sea shortly after setting off to visit the Russian front. His post as Secretary for War was taken by Lloyd George, who like Churchill was of the ' Easterner ' persuasion in matters of strategy, and believed that attacks on the western front were doomed to failure. But the control of strategy was now vested in the hands of the military leaders, Haig and Robertson, both of whom were confirmed ' Westerners '.

As the year went on, impatience began to grow with the failure of the Government to lead rather than to follow public opinion in new measures for the prosecution of the war. Criticism concentrated this time on the Prime Minister himself, who seemed to lack the vigour and drive necessary for the emergency. Asquith had maintained the system of referring all important matters to the full Cabinet, and under his chairmanship too many questions which provoked disagreements in that body were shelved rather than immediately decided in one way or another. Asquith's leading critics were Lloyd George, Sir Edward Carson, and Max Aitken, the owner of the *Daily Express*, and they were supported by Harmsworth, now Lord Northcliffe, who owned both *The Times* and the *Daily Mail*. In November this formidable combination received the support of Bonar Law, and this was decisive, for he was the leader of the Conservative Party. They proceeded to submit demands to Asquith for the establishment of a War Council under Lloyd George's chairmanship. Asquith, if he remained Prime Minister, was to be divorced from the effective control of the war effort. After a few days of crisis, in the course of which Asquith came to believe that he had been cruelly deceived by Lloyd George, the premiership passed to the latter, who instituted a new Coalition Government.

In negotiating with Asquith, Lloyd George had maintained that the premiership should be separated from the direction of the war, because both were full-time jobs. But he at once proceeded to combine these two functions in his own person, and it was obvious that what he had really objected to was

Asquith's lack of vigour rather than his combination of responsibilities. Nevertheless considerable institutional changes were now made : there was to be a small War Cabinet, largely free from departmental responsibilities and thus available for almost daily session ; it was to consist of Lloyd George himself, Bonar Law, who was also to be Chancellor of the Exchequer, and three Ministers without portfolio—Milner, Curzon, and Arthur Henderson. The last-named was brought in to represent Labour, to whose industrial power Lloyd George was in reality making this concession. For the first time minutes were to be taken of Cabinet meetings, and a Cabinet Secretariat was set up under Sir Maurice Hankey. Various measures to extend the powers of the state were promised by the new Prime Minister, including the taking over of the coal mines—this to avert the extension of industrial unrest such as had already manifested itself in South Wales. A number of new Ministries were established to deal with the dangers of the submarine blockade, and into these Lloyd George put the best administrators he could think of—for the most part business men, such as Sir J. P. Maclay as Shipping Controller and Lord Devonport as Food Controller. In military strategy, however, his powers remained limited : he was in no position to replace Haig or to insist on any strong ' Easterner ' policy such as he would have liked. In February 1917 he tried to force Haig into subordination to Nivelle, the new French Commander-in-Chief, but he failed to make this a permanent arrangement ; the episode merely led to great mistrust between Prime Minister and British Commander-in-Chief, for Haig disapproved of Lloyd George's methods quite as much as of his proposals. Lloyd George for his part remained critical of the prevailing military strategy, especially after the costly failure of Passchendaele. In the winter of 1917–18 he did his best to thwart Haig's plans for an offensive by deliberately starving him of troops, which were held back in Britain. In view of the threat of a German offensive this policy was highly dangerous, and even Churchill, the keenest of the ' Easterners ', who was now back in the Government as Minister of Munitions, pleaded with him to reinforce Haig. Meanwhile Lloyd George was also seeking to limit Haig's authority through the Inter-Allied Supreme War Council at

Versailles, which had been set up as an advisory body in November 1917. He sought to give this body executive powers, and to provide it with a reserve of British and French divisions to anticipate a German offensive.

A severe crisis in the military command now took place : on the one side were Haig and Robertson, the Chief of the Imperial General Staff, who wished to maintain their existing control of the army in France ; on the other side were Lloyd George and General Sir Henry Wilson, whom he had appointed as military representative on the Supreme War Council. The crisis came to public notice in February 1918 with the publication in the *Morning Post* of information provided by Robertson's assistant, Sir Frederick Maurice. Lloyd George replaced Robertson with Wilson as Chief of the Imperial General Staff and set on foot a prosecution of the editor and military correspondent of the *Morning Post* for their indiscretions. Two months later the whole controversy was rendered obsolete by the German offensive, which induced Haig as a crisis measure to accept Foch, the French representative at Versailles, as Generalissimo of the whole western front. But Maurice in a letter to the *Morning Post* again attacked Lloyd George for starving the front of men, and this led to a parliamentary challenge to the Prime Minister by Asquith. Lloyd George defended himself in a brilliant speech, and the great bulk of the Conservative Party supported him ; but the Liberals divided almost equally between the Prime Minister and their own party leader—a division that was to have permanent effects on the future of British Liberalism.

In other spheres Lloyd George was more completely in control, but many situations occurred to test his remarkable powers of negotiation and persuasion. He had to drive a very heterogeneous team, consisting of members from every political party except the Irish. The Labour Party, and to a lesser extent the Liberals, became increasingly anxious as the war continued for some formulation of peace aims ; the overthrow of Russian Czarism, and the entry of America into the war, aroused their sense of idealism and their enthusiasm for a world reshaped on the lines of liberal democracy. The Conservatives for the most part simply wanted to ensure the complete defeat of the enemy, and very few of them believed in the possibility of a negotiated peace. Lloyd George himself was a believer in complete military victory—the 'knock-out blow'—but he saw the value of the ideological approach, and in the summer of 1917 he sent Arthur Henderson to make contact with the Kerensky régime in Russia, and to see what could be done to keep the Russians in the war. Henderson became convinced that it was necessary to establish a common agreement with the Russians on the subject of war aims, and he favoured a move to hold a Socialist and Labour Congress at Stockholm, at which German delegates would appear. This was too much for the Conservative members of the War Cabinet, and Lloyd George accepted their view. After being kept waiting outside the door while the subject was under discussion by the rest of the War Cabinet—the 'doormat incident'—Henderson resigned, and was replaced by another Labour leader, George Barnes. Superficially the matter had been treated as a personal one between Lloyd George and Henderson ; and Labour support for the Coalition continued. In practice, however, the situation was considerably altered, for Henderson was much the most important personality in the Labour Party at this time. He now began to work out the lines of an alternative foreign policy, for which he increasingly drew the support of the members of his party, trade union and Socialist alike. This policy entailed the formulation of war aims as a basis for negotiation with the enemy : there were to be no annexations ; a League of Nations was to be set up ; colonial territories were to be regarded as the common responsibility of the more advanced nations.

This pressure from the Labour Party, with its great influence on the industrial workers, combined with the attitude of President Wilson himself, slowly propelled Lloyd George in the direction of the formulation of war aims. Hindered as he was by the obligations of earlier agreements with the European allies, he ensured that his declaration, made on 5th January 1918, was only in the vaguest terms. It was however not incompatible with the much more specific Fourteen Points, enunciated independently by the American President a few days later, and appealed to by the German Government as a basis for peace negotiation at the time of the armistice in November.

In co-ordinating policy with the Dominions, Lloyd George
hit upon a happy if unusual system. In 1917, and again in
1918, he summoned the Dominion Prime Ministers to London,
on the inducement of participating in the sessions of the War
Cabinet. At these meetings Lloyd George discussed with the
Dominion leaders the larger questions of strategy and post-
war reconstruction, and he received much help in return,
including the wise counsel of General Smuts, the Prime
Minister of South Africa.

Lloyd George's personal qualities had made him the indispensable political leader for the nation in wartime. His
administrative ability, his skill as a negotiator, and his fertile
and inventive brain were combined with great oratorical
powers and a wonderful sense of political timing. His principal weakness was perhaps a necessary concomitant of his
greatest qualities : a lack of loyalty to his colleagues and
subordinates gave rise to a good deal of suspicion and mistrust,
necessary though it may have been for the most efficient
conduct of the war. This ruthlessness, which alienated his
old leader Asquith and united in hostility to him such diverse
figures as Haig and Arthur Henderson, no doubt did much to
win the war, as it also did much to ruin the Liberal Party and
finally to drive Lloyd George himself into the political
wilderness.

*

The war was responsible for a great deal of social change,
but this took place gradually. After the patriotic enthusiasm
which hailed the actual outbreak of war, the immediate slogan
was ' business as usual '. It was hoped thereby to minimise
the dislocation of trade, and so prevent any aggravation to the
unemployment which had already developed in some quarters.
But there was no way of averting a sharp rise in prices as
Britain left the gold standard and became dependent once and
for all on paper currency instead of gold for the one pound
and ten shilling denominations. To alleviate suffering, a
voluntary fund was at once launched and soon reached a
figure of several hundred thousand pounds.

The general view prevailed in 1914 that the war could not
last more than a few months. The early censorship of news,

clumsy as it was, encouraged the circulation of optimistic rumours : the British troops at Mons, it was reported, had been saved by the appearance of an angel ; Russian reinforcements were coming to the western front, and various witnesses claimed to have seen them travelling through Britain with the snow still on their boots. After a few months, however, the hope of a speedy end to the war began to fade. The flow of casualties from the western front played a part in this ; and the Belgian refugees who crowded into Britain as their country was occupied were visible evidence of the advance of the German armies. In December 1914 the immediacy of the enemy threat was brought to England itself by the bombardment of Scarborough by German cruisers ; and in 1915 began a series of air raids by airships, called ' Zeppelins ' after their German designer. These attacks on the homeland did no serious damage except to civilian lives and property, and it was not long before the British public had formed a very low opinion of their opponents' methods of waging war. This low opinion was strengthened by the German introduction of asphyxiating gas on the western front—a weapon speedily adopted by the Allies, who had the prevailing wind in their favour, but not of any great military importance after the introduction of suitable respirators. Even more convincing proof of German barbarism, in the British view, was the torpedoing of liners and merchant ships without warning.

Infuriated by these events, the reaction of the public was violent, indeed hysterical. Persons with German names were immediately assumed to be pro-German ; servants of the state as eminent as Prince Louis of Battenberg, the First Sea Lord, were forced to give up their posts ; and the King himself felt it necessary to deprive the German and Austrian royal families of their British titles, and to change the name of his own family to the more English one of ' Windsor '. After the sinking of the *Lusitania*, in May 1915, so many bakers' shops in London were wrecked because of their German-sounding names that a bread shortage temporarily threatened. And there were frequent false alarms about supposed spies signalling to the Zeppelins, and even tales of enemy agents laying down concrete floors in their houses so as to provide suitable gun emplacements for future use by German invaders.

Naturally the pacifists in the Liberal and Labour Parties who opposed the war were regarded as enemy agents themselves, and their meetings were often broken up. Ramsay Mac-Donald was bitterly attacked in the press and, to his great mortification, was expelled from the Lossiemouth Golf Club.

Gradually it began to be realised that the war necessitated a full mobilisation of the country's resources. The shell shortage of 1915 gave a clear indication of the need for an intensive industrial effort. Unemployment disappeared, wages rose sharply, and the unions were able to drive hard bargains for their concessions in respect of the abandonment of strikes and the dilution of labour. Lloyd George, as Minister of Munitions, dealt skilfully with industrial unrest, which centred on Clydeside and South Wales. He soon became convinced that it was necessary to reduce what he considered to be the excessive consumption of drink. For a time there was talk of the nationalisation of liquor manufacture and supply, and even of prohibition. But in the end a less drastic policy was adopted—a policy of increasing the taxation of beer and spirits and of reducing licensing hours. The King, however, decided to set an example by forbidding intoxicants at his own table until the end of the war. He also made a series of visits to war factories, in order to emphasise the importance of munition work.

Meanwhile the country had been losing heavily as a result of the unplanned use of its manpower resources. The flower of the regular army had been killed or wounded in 1914 ; after them the young men of the more educated classes, who provided a high proportion of Kitchener's army, were sacrificed in their turn. Casualties among junior officers were higher than in any other army : in this way the *élite* of a whole British generation was destroyed. Little attention was paid to the special skill or qualifications that the volunteers might have : in the first year of the war no less than a quarter of a million miners were allowed to join the army. Only gradually in 1915 were certain occupations classified as essential for the nation's welfare ; and the voluntary system, as we have seen, was persisted in until well into 1916. Then, and only then, were the full possibilities of women's contribution to the war effort fully appreciated. Already they had been working in large numbers as nurses for the Voluntary Aid Detachments (V.A.D.s), as canteen workers and as munition workers ; now they took over a multitude of occupations—as bank clerks, railway porters, chauffeurs, even navvies in gas-works. Early in 1916 the Army founded a Women's Auxiliary Army Corps, and the W.A.A.C.s, as they were called, relieved many soldiers for more active service at the front. The Navy also had its Women's Royal Naval Service or ' Wrens '.

In 1917 the crisis caused by the submarine blockade had its effect in further transforming British life. Food supplies began to grow short, and the Food Controller decided to restrict the size of restaurant and hotel meals, and published a variety of warnings to the general public. Suitably high prices were fixed for the production of corn, so as to encourage the breaking up of uncultivated land. But discontent grew in 1917 as the scarcity of food increased and with it the price to the consumer. In the summer Lord Devonport, the first Food Controller, was replaced by Lord Rhondda, who at once introduced a price-control system for basic foods such as bread and potatoes. In August it became necessary for the consumer to register with a retailer in order to obtain sugar. At the end of the year meat began to disappear from the shops altogether ; and early in 1918 a rationing system, with cards, was at last introduced.

It was natural that, with so many shortages, there should be a continuous tendency for prices to rise. It has been calculated that, up to the end of 1917, prices rose by about 27 per cent per annum ; after that the development of more effective price and wage control, together with heavy taxation, slowed down the increase. By the end of the war, however, wholesale prices were 140 per cent above pre-war : this meant that the pound had dropped in value to the equivalent of 8s 3d in pre-war money. In the same period the National Debt increased from £650 million to the staggering total of £7,000 million—an indication that much of the financial burden of the war effort had been postponed to the future in the form of interest charges on this sum. All the same, the proportion of the immediate expense of the war that was met by the taxpayer was larger than in other heavily involved countries. The income of the Exchequer quadrupled between

1914 and 1918, and the maximum rate of income tax rose from 9d to 6s in the pound. In addition to this, super-tax, at a maximum of 4s 6d in the pound, started on incomes of £2,500 ; there were heavy Excess Profits Duties to prevent firms from benefiting too easily from war contracts ; and personal expenditure was tapped by heavy duties on spirits and beer, and special levies on theatre and cinema tickets and on entry to football matches. Those who still had money to spend were faced with an intensive campaign to induce them to invest it in War Bonds or in National Savings, and partly for patriotic reasons, partly because there was little enough to buy anyway, these exhortations proved very successful.

The enormous extension of state control in so many spheres caused a large increase in the size of the Civil Service. Proposals which only a Socialist could have advocated before the war were now readily adopted by all parties for the sake of promoting the war effort. The powers of the state extended everywhere—by the end of the war it not only managed the mines and all the means of transport : it controlled the profits of industry, the wages of the workers, the hours of labour, and the conduct of industrial disputes. Through the Whitley Committee on Industrial Conciliation, which reported in 1917, it sponsored the establishment of joint councils of workers and employers for continuous consultation. It took over innumerable hotels and houses to accommodate its own bureaucracy, and where this was not possible it proliferated into innumerable temporary huts. The greatest extension of state powers took place in 1917 when, partly in order to secure the full support of Labour, Lloyd George established Ministries of Food, of Pensions, of Labour, and of Blockade. These developments, which the Socialists had for so long advocated, were to a considerable extent a recognition of the political claims of the labour force, resulting from its industrial importance.

In 1918 two further new ministries were established, each pointing to the future in its own fashion. One of them was the Air Ministry, which was necessitated by the growing importance of the air weapon and the inconvenience of dividing its development between the Army and the Navy. Public opinion had long been impressed with the importance of aerial warfare ; the air raids had seen to that. In March

1916 a Mr Pemberton Billing was elected to Parliament at a by-election solely on the platform of ' a strong air policy '. By the end of 1916 the menace of the clumsy Zeppelin had been ended by the growing efficiency of fast, manoeuvrable heavier-than-air craft, which could easily shoot them down ; but in 1917 German machines of this type were increasingly used for bombing missions over Britain. No great military damage was ever effected by the raids, but public morale was disturbed, and the people of the East End began to develop the habit of crowding into the underground tube stations on moonlit nights, when raids were expected. Meanwhile the importance of air superiority over the battle fronts, as a means of discovering the enemy's intentions and concealing one's own, was increasingly recognised. The Royal Flying Corps and the Royal Naval Air Service were therefore united into the Royal Air Force, and Lord Rothermere, brother of Lord Northcliffe, became the first Minister for Air.

The other ministry created in the last year of war was the Ministry of Reconstruction which, though not of much significance for what it actually did, was nevertheless symbolic of a growing interest in social developments. More definite evidence of the same interest was provided by the enactment of particular reforms. The new Representation Act of 1918 gave the vote to all men over 21 and to women aged 30 and over, and replaced the old special franchises with a single residential system supplemented only by a business and a university vote. The constituency boundaries were redrawn, mostly to form one-member constituencies, and a number of old anomalies were removed : all voting was henceforth to be done on the same day, and returning officers' expenses were to be paid by the Treasury instead of by the candidates. The Act enfranchised a total of eight million new voters, including six million women. Another reform of almost equal significance—of greater significance, if it had been carried out in full—was the Education Act sponsored by H. A. L. Fisher, the university don appointed by Lloyd George to the Board of Education. This provided for entirely free elementary education to the age of 14, and further part-time education to the age of 18. Arrangements were also made for the extension of higher education, for physical training in schools, and for the establishment of nursery schools for children under the normal school age.

These Acts were at least an earnest of the intention to rebuild the country after the war better than it had previously been—the intention so graphically expressed, as usual, by the Prime Minister himself when he spoke of ' a country fit for heroes to live in '. These aspirations on the part of the politicians were necessary indeed to counter the growing war-weariness, expressed in apathy and cynicism, which was beginning to affect the nation's combatants and its labour force, and which can be measured, for instance, by the contrast between the war poetry of Rupert Brooke (who died on war service in 1915) and that written later by Wilfred Owen or Siegfried Sassoon. In 1918 Haig's words in his ' Backs to the Wall ' message at the height of the German offensive had a more general significance for the whole nation : ' Many of us are now tired. To those I would say that victory will belong to the side which holds out the longest.' Hopes for the future bolstered up the British morale in those last vital months. But the strain was great, and when the maroons sounded in London to announce the signing of the armistice, the pre-dominant reaction was not the elation of triumph but the relief of exhaustion.

Plate 7 THE ALLIED VICTORY.   (*Above*) The German Fleet steaming towards Scotland to surrender, 1918.   (*Below*) King George V and the Prince of Wales (later King Edward VIII) greeting Lloyd George on his return from the Versailles Peace Conference, 1919.

Plate 8 LIBERAL LEADERSHIP. Asquith in 1923 with his daughter, Mrs (later Lady Violet) Bonham-Carter.

5 Post-war Retrenchment, 1918-29

BRITAIN'S object in entering the war had been to secure herself against the threat of a predominant European power. She was not otherwise very interested in the problems of Europe, and it had been a profoundly shocking experience to her people to have been involved in several years of bitter, continuous warfare on the Continent. The post-war decade witnessed her attempt to withdraw from the European scene so as to cope with the new problems of her world position and the need for a consolidation of her imperial responsibilities.

The peace treaty with Germany was drawn up at Versailles under the direction of a Council of Four—Lloyd George, Clemenceau, Wilson, and Orlando, the leaders of Britain, France, the United States, and Italy respectively. Lloyd George had secured a new lease on the office of Prime Minister by winning a hasty general election fought before the end of 1918, and although he had made many verbal assurances of his intention to make Germany pay to the limit of her resources, he had every intention of maintaining a flexible approach to the practical problems of the settlement. On most issues he took a position somewhere between that of Wilson, who wanted a peace based so far as possible on the liberal principles of his Fourteen Points, including self-determination of peoples and no annexations, and that of Clemenceau, who was anxious only to secure the subjection of Germany and the extraction from her of the maximum amount of reparations. The situation resulting from the armistice, by which the Allies secured effective military control of Germany, guaranteed the acceptance of any terms that the victors could agree upon ; and Wilson was gradually forced to recognise this. In return for his agreement to a number of punitive measures, including the unilateral disarmament of Germany and her acceptance of an unlimited bill for reparations, Wilson secured the incorporation in the peace treaty of the establishment of the League of Nations, together with the enumeration of a number of important general principles of international justice. To the defeated these decisions naturally assumed a somewhat hypocritical appearance : Britain, for instance, though not interested in annexations in Europe, obtained considerable advantages from the severe restrictions placed on German naval building—no submarines and no warships of over 10,000 tons ; and although Britain formally annexed no territory, she secured League of Nations ' mandates ' which entrusted her with the government of the bulk of the former German colonies and the Turkish possessions in the Middle East. The map of Europe was now redrawn in order to constitute a number of new nations out of the old empires—Poland, Czechoslovakia, Yugoslavia, and an enlarged Rumania. Austria and Hungary, now separate states, were drastically reduced in size, and a tentative move to unite Austria with Germany was forbidden. Germany herself lost Alsace and Lorraine to France and the Saar to semi-permanent French occupation ; and the Polish corridor to the newly constituted free state of Danzig cut her main body from the remnant of East Prussia.

The boundaries of the new Russia were beyond the powers of the Allies to determine. In 1918 they had intervened in Russia to oppose the Bolsheviks, and to support the ' White Russian ' generals, in the hope that a return of the old régime might bring Russia back into the war. British bases, with troops to guard them, had thus been established at Archangel and Murmansk and in the Caucasus. But the main object of the intervention had disappeared with the end of the war against Germany ; much larger forces would have been necessary to turn the scales against the Bolsheviks ; and accordingly in the course of 1919 the Allies, war-weary as they were, accepted the situation and withdrew their troops. French support of the Polish armies prevented the Bolsheviks from carrying their revolution into eastern Europe or even securing the pre-war boundaries of the Russian Empire. Poland won for herself an extended eastern frontier, and the small independent states of Estonia, Latvia, and Lithuania were established on the Baltic coast.

Turkey also presented a serious challenge to the Allies, for under her nationalist leader, Mustafa Kemal, she refused to accept the occupation by Greece of half of Anatolia, and was only held back from an attack upon Allied forces at the Dardanelles by an ultimatum from Lloyd George in 1922 (the Chanak crisis). A final settlement was made by the Treaty of Lausanne in 1923.

Such were the main territorial settlements arising from the war. While they were being concluded, the victorious powers were finding much to disagree about among themselves. The greatest blow to the future of the agreements was dealt by the refusal of the American Senate to accept either the Versailles Treaty or the establishment of the League of Nations. This led to the abrupt withdrawal of the United States from all responsibility for the European settlement, and it encouraged disagreements between France and Britain, for France became the more anxious to guarantee her own security by the subjection of Germany, while Britain became the keener to withdraw from any undertakings to assist in the maintenance of the French position. Britain and the United States had made a tentative agreement to guarantee the French frontiers, but the American failure to confirm it provided the British Government with an opportunity to escape from her own share of the responsibility.

Seriously concerned as they were over the swollen military expenditures that persisted into peace time, the immediate object of Britain and the United States came to be to achieve some sort of agreement between the world's naval powers for a limitation of their building programmes. By the Treaty of Washington, 1922, Britain agreed to parity with the United States but secured a limitation of Japanese tonnage to 60 per cent, and of French and Italian to 35 per cent, of her own tonnage. She also agreed, under American pressure, to renounce the Anglo-Japanese alliance and to substitute for it a four-power pact of Britain, America, Japan, and France, for the stabilisation of the Pacific area. In this way Britain was accepting the predominance of the United States, not only in the waters adjacent to the American continent, but also in the Far East. She was also excluding from the bounds of strategical hypothesis the possibility of a conflict between herself and the United States.

With the achievement of these arrangements between the naval powers, the pacification of Europe remained the outstanding problem. With Russia in the position of an international outlaw owing to her espousal of the doctrine of world revolution, it was all the more necessary to bring Germany into some form of association with the victorious powers, provided this could be done without upsetting the French insistence upon military safeguards against the former enemy. A solution was found in 1925 by the Treaty of Locarno, under which the frontier between France and Germany was guaranteed by Britain and Italy. In this way Britain undertook the responsibility for French security which she had earlier rejected, although in the existing disarmed state of Germany no special military provisions seemed to be required. The British occupation force which had been installed in the Rhineland after the war was finally withdrawn in 1929.

After this the main problems that disturbed international relations were economic ones—that of reparations from Germany and, associated with it, the vexed question of the inter-Allied war debts. The attempt to secure reparations from Germany had been largely responsible for that country's financial collapse in 1922, which in turn led to a French occupation of the Ruhr in 1923 in a futile attempt to coerce the German Government. By this time British and American opinion, influenced by a certain sense of war-guilt as well as by the practical economist's arguments expressed in J. M. Keynes's *Economic Consequences of the Peace* (1919), began to have serious doubts about the merits of a policy of saddling Germany with a vast reparations bill.

Part of the difficulty arose from the fact that France needed the reparations in order to pay her war debts to other countries, particularly to Britain and America. Britain, for her part, though a creditor of her allies to the extent of some £1,740 million (of which £568 million had been lent to Russia, and was now irrecoverable), in her turn owed the United States some £842 million, and could not afford to be very generous to her debtors without serious danger to her balance of pay-

ments. The United States, which was the creditor of her
former allies to the extent of £2,000 million, could alone afford
to be generous, and it was largely American money that was
lent to Germany to rebuild her shattered finances and to put
her in a position to resume a certain level of reparations
payments. This loan (the Dawes Loan, 1924) was responsible
for a considerable economic recovery by Germany, which
lasted for the remainder of the decade.

There was no doubt that the United States had replaced
Britain as the principal source of foreign investment for the
rest of the world. Britain had in fact sold about a quarter of
her foreign investments during the war, in order to secure
supplies, and the bulk of these had gone to the United States.
Although three-quarters of her foreign investments still
remained, her balance of payments was not such as to enable
her to add extensively to their total. The war itself had
dislocated her foreign trade and had thus given many of her
competitors, especially the neutral countries, an opportunity
to win her markets. Some of the less-developed countries
with which she traded had been forced to develop their own
industries, and having done so were naturally reluctant to
resume their pre-war trade with Britain on the old basis.
There was also the important fact that the staple exports of
Britain, coal and textiles, were commodities whose share of
total world trade was in rapid decline. British coal exports
declined from 82 million tons in 1907 to 70 million tons in
1930, owing to the loss of such markets as Italy, now rapidly
developing its hydro-electric resources ; and British cotton
exports declined in the same period from £105 million to
£86 million, and their proportion in respect of total British
manufactured exports dropped from 31 per cent to 23·5 per
cent. These figures indicate the principal cause of the chronic
depression which affected the coal and textile industries in
these years.

There were of course new industries which were now
developing rapidly, many of them having been stimulated by
the needs of war. Prominent among them were the electrical
and chemical industries and the manufacture of motor cars
and aircraft. But their products, though in demand at home,
could not yet compete satisfactorily in foreign markets with

the manufactures of other nations. America, former neutral countries such as Holland and Switzerland, and even the defeated Germany, were outstripping Britain in the new industries. The result was that total exports in the 1920's remained at not much more than 80 per cent of the pre-war figure, and the unemployment figures were never much less than a million throughout the decade. Nor was this due to a reduction in total world trade : the fact was that Britain's share of the total of all nations' exports had fallen from over 13 per cent in 1913 to under 11 per cent in 1929 ; and the United States, which had taken the lead in so many other respects, had also replaced Britain as the chief exporting nation of the world.

At the same time Britain's share of world imports did not decline, but actually increased. This was largely due to increased imports of meat, dairy produce, and fruit—evidence of the still rising standard of living of the people—and to the growing demand for newer raw materials such as petroleum and rubber. Naturally this led to a serious adverse balance of visible trade, which would have had immediate awkward consequences were it not for two favourable factors. One of these was the world glut in primary products, which caused imported food and raw materials to be very inexpensive in relation to manufactured exports. This meant that the ' terms of trade ' were tilted in Britain's favour : and although it also meant that in the long run the primary producing countries might be unable to buy much of Britain's exports owing to their poverty, in the short run it helped considerably to improve Britain's trading balance. The second factor was the existence of Britain's overseas investments and her leading role in the spheres of insurance, shipping, and other commercial and financial services for foreign customers. The profits of this activity, sometimes known as ' invisible exports ', served to cover the remaining deficit between ' visible ' exports and imports. But, as we have seen, there was no large surplus left over to supply the basis for fresh foreign lending on the pattern of the pre-war years. In this sense Britain was now beginning to live on her past.

Since the United States was now the principal foreign lender, it was natural that Wall Street, rather than the City of London, should become the principal financial centre of the world. But the City remained the centre of world insurance, and there were many financial services that it could still perform for foreign firms and governments. To encourage the latter to maintain and to increase their use of the London money market, Winston Churchill as Chancellor of the Exchequer in 1925 returned to the gold standard, which meant restoring the pound to its pre-war value. This was not done without considerable strain, and it had a weakening effect on British ' visible ' exports, which became over-priced in the world market. Exporters could see no solution to the problem of how to reduce costs except by reduction of wage levels, and their attempts to secure this led to industrial unrest. In fact wages were not substantially reduced, and export prices remained high, with a continued adverse effect upon their volume. Thus Britain could not escape from a high level of unemployment in her export trades even in the later 1920's, when America and many other countries including Germany were experiencing an industrial boom.

The weakened world position of Britain was paralleled by an increased confidence and independence on the part of the self-governing Dominions. As a result of their contributions to the war effort they had secured separate representation at the peace conference and as members of the League of Nations. Several of them had been entrusted with ex-enemy territory to administer under League mandates. The Chanak incident in 1922 showed that they were no longer willing to give automatic military support to British diplomacy, for Lloyd George's hurried demand for troops met in most cases with a dusty answer. Consequently, when in 1925 Britain undertook military obligations in Europe under the Locarno Pact, it was specifically agreed that the obligation did not extend to the Dominions. To ensure that they could conduct their own diplomacy, the Dominions now began to appoint diplomatic representatives of their own, Canada leading the way by sending an ambassador to Washington in 1927. An Imperial Conference which met in London in 1926 decided to give legal effect to the status of equality with the mother-country which the Dominions had now assumed, and accordingly legislation to this effect was prepared, approved by the

Imperial Conference of 1930, and enacted in the form of the Statute of Westminster, 1931.

The number of the Dominions had been increased by the inclusion under somewhat special circumstances of the Irish Free State. The 1918 General Election had seen 73 members of Sinn Fein, the extreme nationalist organisation, successful at the polls. This group refused to appear at Westminster but instead constituted itself as the Parliament of Ireland, sitting in Dublin. Gradually this self-appointed administration came into armed conflict with the British Government through the agency of their respective armed forces, the Irish Republican Army and the Royal Irish Constabulary. The latter had been hastily reinforced by specially recruited military veterans, who wore a partly khaki uniform and were known as the ' Black and Tans '. The Black and Tans were lacking in the discipline necessary for a police force, and they matched the nationalist terrorism of the I.R.A. with an equally savage terrorism of their own. Gradually guerrilla warfare developed on a scale and with a barbarism on both sides that was deeply shocking to British opinion, and eventually brought the recognition that some form of Home Rule, with suitable safeguards for Ulster, was inevitable. At the end of 1921 Lloyd George and a number of his Cabinet colleagues succeeded in negotiating an agreement with the Sinn Fein leaders : an Irish Free State, excluding six counties of Ulster, was to be established ; it was to have complete autonomy within the British Commonwealth, but was to grant to Britain the use of certain ports for purposes of naval defence and was to assume certain financial obligations. The agreement was not accepted in Ireland without the greatest difficulty : civil war broke out between the pro-treaty and anti-treaty factions of the I.R.A. But in 1922 the Free State was constituted, and Ireland settled down to an uneasy peace which was a vast improvement on the years of bitter conflict that had disturbed the country for so many years. Instead of over a hundred Irish M.P.s, Westminster saw now only the thirteen representatives of the six counties, which also had their own parliament at Belfast for domestic purposes.

In other parts of the Empire Britain began to move slowly towards a policy of limiting her own responsibilities and encouraging the development of local autonomy. The tenta-

tive character of the approach was matched by the backward-
ness of the political development of the non-European peoples.
Only in India and in Egypt, and among the Indian immigrants
to East Africa, were there active nationalist movements.   In
Egypt the Government met with an intransigent opposition
with which it was unable to come to terms : instead in 1922
it unilaterally recognised nominal Egyptian independence but
reserved for its own supervision the defence of Egypt and the
Suez Canal, and also the administration of the Sudan.   Continued Egyptian hostility led to a tightening of British control
in the later years of the decade.   In Kenya difficulties arose
between the European and the Indian settlers, and the Colonial
Office was forced to state a policy for the colony.   By asserting
the interest of the native population as ' paramount ' it reserved
for itself the effective control for a long time to come.

But the greatest test of empire, as always, was India, where
the Congress party was growing in stature as the representative
of nationalism.   India's contributions to the war effort had
encouraged the Cabinet to make a declaration in 1917 that its
aim was the achievement of responsible government ; and by
a somewhat anomalous concession India was accorded separate
representation at Versailles and in the League of Nations as if
she were an independent state.   The Government of India Act,
1919, based on the Montagu-Chelmsford Report of the previous year, introduced a system of ' dyarchy ' by which the
government was divided between elected representatives and
officials.   The atmosphere in which this experiment was initiated was not improved by the so-called ' Amritsar massacre ',
when a body of troops under General Dyer fired on a threatening but unarmed mob, killing 379 people.   Mahatma Gandhi,
the Congress leader, launched a campaign for complete independence, which was to be achieved by non-violent ' civil
disobedience ' and the use of the boycott.   He was arrested
and sent to prison for six years.   But it was clear that Indian
nationalism would soon present a test for British statesmanship
comparable in its complexity with the Irish problem, though
on the enormously larger scale of a sub-continent with three
hundred million inhabitants.

★

The end of the war did not see the immediate dissolution of the war-time Coalition, for Lloyd George's success at the General Election of December 1918 gave it a fresh lease of life. The election was long overdue, for the Parliament elected in December 1910 had perpetuated its own existence during the war by special legislation. But by precipitating it in the very month after the armistice, Lloyd George ensured that it would be fought upon his record as the architect of victory. He had the united support of the Conservative Party, whose leader Bonar Law was the closest of his colleagues, and also of a considerable proportion of the Liberal Party. To the candidates of these two groups he gave his personal endorsement in the form of a letter signed by himself and Bonar Law—the ' coupon ' as Asquith called it. Independent of the ' coupon ' and in opposition to its candidates were Asquith's supporters, constituting the official Liberal Party, and also the Labour Party, which had decided by majority vote to withdraw from the Coalition.

As might be expected, the election was fought in a highly emotional atmosphere. Lloyd George and his colleagues were forced to promise harsh treatment of the defeated enemy, and the opponents of the war in the Liberal and Labour Parties had to face the bitterest hostility. With a weak and divided opposition the result was never in doubt ; the only question was how large a majority the Coalition would secure. In the event it had 474 members of the new House, of whom 338 were Conservatives and 136 Liberals. The Labour Party returned with 57 members and the Asquith Liberals with 26. A number of independents were also elected, together with 7 Irish Nationalists of the old type and no less than 73 Sinn Fein members, who, as we have seen, refused to take their seats. The most striking feature of the results was, of course, the disintegration of the Liberal Party. This enabled the Conservatives to obtain a clear majority of the House, and thus to exert an increasing influence on the conduct of policy. It also gave added significance to the continued growth of the Labour Party, which now became the official Opposition. It was unfortunate that the Labour Party, though increased in numbers, was virtually leaderless, for Arthur Henderson as well as the pacifist leaders MacDonald and Snowden had been

defeated. William Adamson, a Scottish miner, was elected
as interim leader of the party.

The new Government was little changed from the old.
With the exception of Winston Churchill, most of Lloyd
George's leading colleagues were Conservatives : Bonar Law,
Austen Chamberlain, F. E. Smith—now Lord Birkenhead—
and Balfour. Lloyd George continued to govern through a
small informal group of leading ministers rather than through
the reconstituted official Cabinet of twenty members. His
personal control was strengthened by the maintenance of the
Prime Minister's Secretariat and the Cabinet Secretariat, both
of them wartime creations. A number of the new ministries
continued in existence—those of Transport, Labour, Pensions,
and Air. The Civil Service remained at more than twice the
pre-war level in numbers ; and the permanent powers of the
state were increased by legislation. By the Housing and Town
Planning Act of 1919 the new Ministry of Health (formerly
the Local Government Board) was given powers to assist local
government housing projects with state subsidies ; and by the
Unemployment Insurance Act of 1920 nearly all wage-earners
were brought into the existing national scheme, with provision
for dependents.

But neither the country as a whole nor the Conservative
Party in the Commons wished to see any general maintenance
of strong state powers. In 1919 discontent in the forces com-
pelled the Government to speed up its demobilisation plans,
so that four million men were released by the end of the year.
Women were not allowed to retain the jobs that they had
undertaken in war time, and by 1921 the proportion of women
in employment was actually less than in 1911. This fact, and
the immediate post-war boom, enabled the men to be rapidly
drawn back into industry and commerce. Soon there was a
demand for the abandonment of all controls and projects of
nationalisation. The Government largely gave way to the
pressure, abandoning the various schemes worked out by the
Ministry of Reconstruction, and allowing industrial and commercial controls to expire. War-surplus goods and national
factories were disposed of, and by the beginning of 1921 only
the mines and the railways remained under government
control. In that year the railways were returned to private

hands, though not to the 120 companies which had existed before the war : these were consolidated into four, the Great Western ; the London, Midland and Scottish ; the London and North-Eastern ; and the Southern. Then in the course of the year the boom turned into a slump, and the demands for the freeing of private industry were transformed into attacks on taxation and government expenditure. Sir Eric Geddes was put in charge of a committee to recommend government economics, and its recommendations were so extensive as to earn it the title of the ' Geddes axe '. Among the victims of the ' Geddes axe ' was the Fisher Education Act of 1918, which became almost entirely a dead letter.

The most difficult problem for the Government was that of dealing with the future of the mines. The miners demanded and expected nationalisation, and in 1919 Lloyd George had only staved off a strike on this issue by appointing a special commission of inquiry. The majority of the commission, including its chairman, Sir John Sankey, recommended nationalisation, but the Government rejected the recommendation. Temporary wage increases postponed the threatening crisis until 1921, but in that year the coal export market collapsed, owing to German reparations deliveries and the recovery of the European coalfields. The Government, faced with the prospect of heavy losses on continued operation of the mines, insisted on immediate decontrol ; and the mine-owners felt it necessary to make substantial cuts in wages. A strike ensued in April 1921, and the miners invoked the aid of their allies in the ' Triple Alliance ', the railwaymen and transport workers. On Friday, 15th April, the miners' refusal of a temporary offer by Lloyd George gave these two allies an opportunity to withdraw their support—an event which caused this day to become known in the labour movement as ' Black Friday '. Thus an almost general strike was averted ; the miners, left on their own, acknowledged defeat in July ; and their wages were reduced, in some areas very sharply. Their bitter resentment was left as a legacy for the future.

With the appearance of slump conditions and heavy industrial unemployment, the question of Tariff Reform again came to the fore, and it soon threatened to divide the Coalition supporters. The idea of ' fusion ', of uniting all the Coalition supporters in one party, was already fading in 1920, and Bonar Law's withdrawal from office in 1921 owing to ill health weakened the Government still further. Lloyd George continued to receive the support of the ablest Conservative leaders —Austen Chamberlain, Birkenhead, Balfour—but the Chanak crisis in the autumn of 1922 angered the Conservative rank and file and caused Curzon, who was Foreign Secretary, to resign. Bonar Law, now in better health, attended a meeting of Conservative M.P.s at the Carlton Club and threw in his weight in support of a resolution demanding the end of the Coalition. The resolution was carried with a large majority, and Lloyd George at once resigned.

Bonar Law now formed an exclusively Conservative Government, with Curzon again at the Foreign Office and Stanley Baldwin as Chancellor of the Exchequer. The ablest Conservative leaders, however, stayed out of his Cabinet, aggrieved as they were by the break-up of the Coalition. Bonar Law almost immediately sought a general election, and went to the country under the slogan of ' tranquillity and freedom from adventures and commitments at home and abroad '—obviously an effective phrase to use to a war-weary nation, but one that glossed over the real difference between the parties, not to say the real problems facing the nation. In the result the Conservatives secured a clear majority with 347 seats ; the Lloyd George Liberals lost heavily and returned only 57 strong ; the Asquith Liberals advanced to 60 ; and the Labour Party made a sensational advance to a total of 142. For the first time the size of the Labour Party thus exceeded that of the Liberal factions put together. Inside the Labour Party the I.L.P. pacifists returned in large numbers, and, with the assistance of a strong group of left-wingers from ' Red Clydeside ', Ramsay MacDonald was re-elected to the leadership of the parliamentary party which he had resigned in 1914.

Bonar Law was not able to enjoy his election success for long : in May 1923 failing health again caused his retirement, and he died a few months later. The King, faced with a choice between Curzon and Baldwin, was advised by the other Conservative leaders to send for Baldwin, on the grounds that it would be unsuitable to have a Prime Minister in the

Lords. Such a consideration, inconceivable in Queen Victoria's time, was largely due to the new importance of the Labour Party, which had almost no spokesmen in the Lords. Baldwin, with an eye to the reconciliation of the factions within his party, appointed Neville Chamberlain, Austen's younger brother, as Chancellor of the Exchequer ; and with the same object he also announced his conversion to Tariff Reform, and before the end of 1923 precipitated a general election on this issue. Although the move helped to reunite the party, it resulted in defeat at the polls : the Conservative Party sank to 258 ; the Liberals, now fighting together on the platform of free trade, numbered 158 ; and the Labour Party continued its rapid rise by winning 191 seats.

Since the electors had rejected the Conservatives, and since the Labour Party was the larger of the two free-trade parties, it was natural that it should take office with the support of the other. Thus the first Labour Government came into existence, with Ramsay MacDonald as Prime Minister. MacDonald had difficulty in finding suitable members of his party for some of the posts of government, and he was forced to bring in several former Liberals or non-party men. He retained the Foreign Office for himself, and appointed his closest colleagues, Snowden, Henderson, Thomas, and Clynes respectively, to the Exchequer, the Home Office, the Colonial Office, and the Privy Seal. But Haldane was brought in as Lord Chancellor, and Lord Chelmsford, a former Viceroy of India, became First Lord of the Admiralty. On the whole it was a moderate Government, effectively designed to disprove Winston Churchill's gibe that Labour was ' not fit to govern '. It could do nothing without Liberal support, so there was no question of introducing a distinctively Socialist programme of legislation ; but in the spheres of foreign policy and social welfare it could hope to make a modest contribution.

These hopes were not unjustified. Although Snowden's budget was marked by a free-trade orthodoxy that commended itself more to the Liberals than to his own party— he repealed the wartime McKenna duties which protected certain struggling British manufactures—a useful Housing Act was passed on the initiative of John Wheatley, the Minister of Health ; and MacDonald's diplomacy undoubtedly played an important part in securing a temporary settlement of the reparations question and an improvement of Franco-German relations. In September 1924 MacDonald personally attended a meeting of the Assembly of the League of Nations, and other ministers helped to draft the ' Geneva Protocol ' which proposed the establishment of permanent machinery for the arbitration of international disputes. The Protocol had not been ratified, however, before the Government fell ; and it was then abandoned.

The most critical sphere of policy for the Labour Government was its relations with Communism. Although averse to Bolshevik methods, the Labour Party had always been anxious to resume normal diplomatic relations with Russia, which had been severed since 1918. This was done on 1st February 1924, and in the following months negotiations took place for commercial and financial agreements. Two treaties were finally initialled in August. But the Conservative Opposition was bitterly hostile to these arrangements, and sought to show that the Government was unduly weak in dealing with Communism. A domestic opportunity soon came their way : in September the Attorney-General withdrew a prosecution against J. R. Campbell, the editor of a small Communist paper, who had been charged with ' incitement to mutiny ' because of an article addressed to the troops. The Conservatives maintained that the prosecution had been withdrawn for political reasons, and they accordingly moved a vote of censure, for which they anticipated Liberal support. MacDonald refused to accept a Liberal compromise in the form of a committee of inquiry, and the result was that the Government was defeated. MacDonald secured a dissolution, and a new general election—the third in two years—took place in October. Just four days before polling, the *Daily Mail* startled its readers by publishing a letter supposedly from the Russian Bolshevik leader Zinoviev to the tiny British Communist Party. The letter gave instructions for the preparation of military insurrection in Britain, and its authenticity, which later fell into considerable doubt, appeared to be confirmed by the fact that the Foreign Office at once protested to the Russian Government about it.

The result of the election was in any case a foregone

conclusion. The electorate, having experienced a Labour Government, was bound to feel that the choice now lay between Conservative and Labour, so that the Liberal Party inevitably lost ground. It lost 116 seats and returned only 42 strong. The Conservatives won much of the Liberal vote, being assisted by Baldwin's pledge not to introduce Tariff Reform, which had proved such an unpopular issue in 1923. With a total of 415 seats the Conservatives won a position of overwhelming strength. The Labour Party, although it lost 42 seats and dropped to a total of 152, had nevertheless increased its popular vote, partly as a result of running more candidates.

Baldwin's second Government was stronger than his first one, for the former Coalition Conservatives now rallied to his leadership and came in to take the high offices to which some of them were accustomed. Austen Chamberlain became Foreign Secretary, Birkenhead Secretary for India; and Baldwin also brought in Churchill as Chancellor of the Exchequer—a surprise move, for Churchill had not been a Conservative since 1903. Events were to show, however, that in the fierce political strife that ensued, the voice of compromise inside the Cabinet was not Churchill's but Baldwin's.

The new Government at first showed great determination in reversing the work of its predecessor. The Geneva Protocol and both the treaties with Russia were abandoned; and some of the backbenchers attempted to cripple the Labour Party by abolishing the trade-union political levy, on which its finances were based. Here, however, they met the opposition of Baldwin, who disclaimed the Bill with the words ' Give peace in our time, O Lord ! ' ; and so the proposal was defeated. But the conflict with the industrial movement of labour could not be avoided. The syndicalist ideas that flourished before and during the war, the disappointment with the failure of the ' Triple Alliance ', and the defeat of the Labour Government, all encouraged the growth of militancy in the trade unions ; and the General Council of the T.U.C., a body constituted for the first time in 1921, was regarded as a suitable leadership for a general strike. The justification for action was the economic unrest which followed the return to the gold standard in 1925, and particularly the special problem of the

Plate 9 PRIME MINISTERS OF THE 1920's. (*Above*) Ramsay MacDonald speaking at a Labour Party meeting, 1924. On his left : Margaret Bondfield, J. H. Thomas, Robert Smillie, Josiah Wedgwood. (*Below*) Stanley Baldwin (seated, second from left) at the Imperial Conference, 1923. Also seated (from the left) : Mackenzie King (Canada), Stanley Bruce (Australia), Lord Salisbury, and General Smuts (South Africa).

Plate 10 THE GENERAL STRIKE, 1926. An armoured car escorting a food convoy.

miners, whose wages were again threatened with reductions, and for whose misfortunes the labour movement felt a special sympathy since ' Black Friday ' of 1921.

Baldwin, like Lloyd George before him, at first succeeded in postponing a conflict with the miners by appointing a Royal Commission.   While the Commission, under Sir Herbert Samuel's chairmanship, was holding its inquiries, the Government prepared measures to deal with a general strike.   It set up an ' Organisation for the Maintenance of Supplies ', to recruit and train volunteer workers ;   and it arrested the leaders of the tiny Communist Party, which it believed would take advantage of a civil conflict for revolutionary purposes. The Samuel Commission reported in March 1926 in favour of a number of lesser reforms, but insisted on an immediate reduction of miners' wages.   This was quite unacceptable to the miners' leaders, who prepared for fresh strike action and called upon the General Council of the T.U.C. for active support.   In this way the crisis was precipitated.   On 30th April the Government assumed emergency powers, and on 4th May the General Strike began.

The following nine days witnessed an astonishing spectacle —of the orderly withdrawal of labour in the transport and other industries, and of the hasty improvisation of essential services by the Government.   In some areas, where the labour movement was weak, life went on much as before.   But in all the major industrial areas the workers behaved with remarkable cohesion, leaving the railway stations and the bus depots in a strange silence of immobility.   The workers used their trades councils or improvised Councils of Action to publicise their case, to organise picketing, and to issue permits for essential supplies ;   the Government appointed local Civil Commissioners, and used volunteers, protected if necessary by police and even by troops, to try to get the services going again.   Countless white-collar workers and students rushed with immense enthusiasm to undertake such interesting tasks as bus-driving or even engine-driving ;   their lack of skill, however, prevented them from building up very effective services.   There were surprisingly few disturbances of the peace, and in some areas football matches took place between the strikers and the police.

Meanwhile the T.U.C. leaders were in great confusion, both as to how to conduct the strike and as to what terms to demand from the Government. Some of them were afraid of losing control of the movement to the extremists of the left wing; and they were soon willing to grasp at the smallest hint of concession on the part of the Government. On 6th May Sir John Simon, a former Attorney-General, caused them some concern by proclaiming the strike illegal and its leaders liable for damages. It was Sir Herbert Samuel, however, who made most impression upon them by offering his services as a negotiator. He drew up a memorandum filling out some of the mining reforms proposed by his Commission, and the General Council accepted it as a basis for negotiation. The miners would not agree to this, but without securing any commitment from the Government the General Council agreed on 12th May to bring the strike to an end. This was in reality a surrender, although the strike was continuing to prove effective throughout the country. Naturally many of the rank and file, and especially the miners, who remained on strike, considered this as a betrayal. And yet the bulk of the workers seemed to realise that this method of attempting to force the Government's hand was a highly dangerous one, as it might lead to civil war. With that realisation came a marked retreat from industrial militancy, which was fortunately encouraged by improving economic conditions in the later 1920's.

The aftermath for the miners, however, was most unhappy : their strike dragged on until the end of the year, but ended in their total defeat and in further wage reductions, accompanied by high unemployment owing to the loss of foreign markets. Not content with their victory, the Government sponsored a Trades Disputes and Trade Union Act (1927), which declared the General Strike illegal and also weakened the Labour Party by establishing ' contracting in ' instead of ' contracting out ' for the trade-union political levy. In addition, a final rupture of Anglo-Russian relations was effected after a somewhat inconclusive police raid on the premises of the Russian Trade Delegation (' Arcos ') in search of evidence of espionage.

Yet the Government was not hostile to social legislation, and through the co-operation of Neville Chamberlain in the

Ministry of Health and Churchill at the Exchequer a good deal was done to improve the pattern of state welfare. A Pensions Act provided for widows and orphans, and for insured workers and their wives at the age of 65. An Unemployed Insurance Act (1927) embodied the report of the Blanesburgh Commission, which recommended some reduction of benefits in order to provide a more regular extension of their payment. And the Local Government Act (1929), also based on the work of commissions, abolished the Poor Law unions and guardians and gave their powers to county and county borough councils. The Treasury was henceforth to make block grants to the local authorities in exchange for the re-rating of industrial property—a change which both made for a more equitable distribution of income among the local authorities and relieved industry of some of its taxation burden. In 1926 the Government also enacted two measures of nationalisation, in spheres where private enterprise threatened to introduce a state of chaos. These were in the electricity supply industry, where the Central Electricity Board was set up, and in broadcasting, where the B.B.C. was given the charter of a public corporation. Finally, in 1928 a new franchise Act gave the vote to women at the age of 21, the same age as for men.

Meanwhile the three political parties were looking to the next general election. The Asquith Liberals, still somewhat hostile to Lloyd George, were forced to accept his leadership when Asquith retired owing to illness in 1926 ; in return Lloyd George applied his large personal political fund to support party candidates, and also set about building an effective and distinctive policy for the party. He had able advisers in this work, notably the economist J. M. Keynes ; and the Liberal ' Yellow Book ', *Britain's Industrial Future*, which was the outcome of their labours, was far-reaching in its advocacy of economic planning and the initiation of public works, to be financed by borrowing. In the Labour Party, Ramsay MacDonald's leadership was under attack from left-wingers in his old group, the I.L.P., where the Glasgow extremist James Maxton had gained ascendancy. The I.L.P., with the help of another able economist, J. A. Hobson, produced an outline programme of expansion called *Socialism in our Time*, which demanded the introduction of a national minimum wage. MacDonald and Snowden refused to accept this policy, and the official Labour Party was limited to making restatements of its rather vague and generalised 1918 programme. As for the Conservatives, it was apparent that many of them were discontented with the studious moderation of their leader, who had been so willing to abandon Tariff Reform when he found it unpopular with the electorate. But Baldwin held the Government together until the middle of its fifth and last permissible year, and in May 1929 went to the country under the somewhat uninspiring, though not altogether unattractive, slogan of ' Safety First '.

★

Britain could never be quite the same again after such an experience as the First World War ; but the differences were more in manners and in the effects of the new technology than in any radical transformation of the underlying social structure. At first, of course, social life was much overshadowed by the aftermath of the war—by the shortage of young men, so many of whom had been killed or crippled ; by the maintenance of various forms of rationing—the last of which, sugar rationing, did not disappear until November 1920 ; and by the shortage of housing, and the prevalence of industrial unrest, which in 1919 even occasioned police strikes. Soon, however, the pleasures of the wealthy began to be restored : the usual London ' season ', the various social events at the older universities (which were swollen with ex-service undergraduates), fox-hunting, and race meetings, and skating at St Moritz. Certainly taxation remained at a high level, in spite of the ' Geddes axe ' : but if death duties caused the break-up of many old estates, there was a new plutocracy that emerged from the war, and which sought admission to society, often with the advantage of ennoblement in the service of the Lloyd George Coalition (there was a good deal of talk about the ' sale of honours ' by the political leaders in return for contributions to party funds). Domestic servants, it seemed, were getting scarcer and more expensive, and there was much to be said for a flat or a smaller house ; but there were still plenty of people—more indeed than ever before—who could afford to send their children to a public school, where they could obtain an education that was socially, if not always intellectually, distinctive.

At the other end of the social scale, the working class emerged from the war with a greater self-confidence, born of the high wages of wartime and of knowledge of their own importance, both on the battlefield and in the factory, for the success of the war. Socialist ideas of various types were more strongly developed among them than ever before : the influence of the Russian revolution encouraged the growth of Marxism, though there were few out-and-out Communists. The Labour Party adopted a Socialist constitution for the first time in 1918 : it was a result of the collaboration of Arthur Henderson with the Fabian Sidney Webb. The Labour College movement emerged as a strong rival in adult education to the Workers' Educational Association, which was not sufficiently ' advanced ' for some ; and, as we have seen, ideas of syndicalism and of ' direct action ' were prevalent, and helped to create the climate of unrest that, fed by wage cuts, unemployment, and disappointment over Government promises, led to the General Strike. A comparison of wage rates and prices shows that even in 1924 the employed worker was on the average 11 per cent better off than in 1914 ; but this statistical advantage was offset to a considerable extent by the existence of widespread unemployment in the basic industries. For the children of the working class, the avenues of social opportunity had widened slightly with the extension of secondary education and the creation of a small number of state scholarships at the universities : but the proposals of the Fisher Act for extending schooling beyond the age of fourteen had perished under the ' Geddes axe ' ; only one in eight of those who attended elementary schools ever reached a grammar school, and only four in a thousand attended a university.

The changes in manners which followed the war nevertheless in many ways created the appearance of a new world. They were largely the result of the war, which had to a great extent emancipated women from the more irksome social restraints. In the post-war years their costume affected a boyish appearance, as if to emphasise their equality with the male sex, and also their freedom from the conventions of the pre-war generation. Hair was cut short, bobbed or worn in an Eton crop ; skirts were short, and hats became small. Women also began to use face-powder, if not lipstick, and would smoke cigarettes in any type of society. Even men's dress began to change in the direction of informality, with the introduction of lighter-coloured wear for off-duty activities, and the wide-bottomed ' Oxford bags ' or grey-flannel trousers now had their vogue. But the greatest changes were in the freedom of social activity and in the wide extension, at least in London society, of parties and dancing, the latter much under American influence. Jazz was popular, and the novel tango, fox-trot, and slow waltz established themselves. The uninhibited and superficial gaiety of the ' bright young things ' satirised by Evelyn Waugh did not, perhaps, extend to a very large pro-portion of the population : but it set a new social norm which shocked the moralists. Unfortunately there is no satisfactory way of gauging public morality, so we cannot say if it suffered as a consequence. One statistic that was quoted was the rise in the divorce rate from a little over 800 a year just before the war to over 4,000 in the later 1920's. But this was still not a very large figure, no doubt because of the strictness of the law and the difficulty of the proceedings involved.

These social changes were reflected most clearly, as might be expected, in the literature and art of the period. The influence of Sigmund Freud's work on the psychology of sex was manifest, especially on the novelists : D. H. Lawrence, who glorified sexual passion, was highly popular ; so too was the younger Aldous Huxley, more versatile but equally unin-hibited. Virginia Woolf, of the Bloomsbury group, made use of a ' stream-of-consciousness ' technique in her work, as in a different way did James Joyce. In poetry a sharp reaction against traditional themes and methods was most apparent in the work of the expatriate American, T. S. Eliot, whose *Waste Land* (1923) seemed symbolic of the post-war era. Of course these authors did not at once win wide acceptance, and much of Lawrence's work was regarded as pornography. Writers in more traditional styles such as Conrad, Arnold Bennett, Thomas Hardy, Galsworthy, W. B. Yeats, Kipling, and Robert Bridges had a wider public.

On the stage the light comedies of Noel Coward best fitted the tone of the period, shocking though they were to some ; Bernard Shaw's social criticism, while also controversial, seemed to be of a pre-war vintage—though his most popular play, *St Joan* (1924), was more serious than usual. In sculpture Jacob Epstein outraged the conventional and the prudish ; in art, Continental painters such as Matisse and Picasso only gradually won acceptance. Architecture, of all the arts, alone remained largely within the bounds of earlier traditions : big public buildings or offices tended to a heavy classical style, while most house-building was imitative and unadventurous.

It was not quite clear yet whether the cinema could be regarded as an art. Its enormous expansion in this period, however, deserves attention. The products of Hollywood dominated the British market, its heroes being Rudolph Valentino, Mary Pickford, and Charlie Chaplin among others. In 1927 an Act was passed to ensure that a quota of all films shown in British cinemas was of British manufacture. This brought into existence several film companies, including Gaumont-British which controlled a chain of cinemas, and Associated British Cinemas. But in the 1920's there was little of quality made in British studios except for a few documentaries. In 1929 there came—from America—the first talking picture, and as a result the industry embarked on a new wave of prosperity. The growth of cinema attendance must have played its part in the remarkable decline in drunkenness since before the war : the convictions for this offence fell from 189,000 in 1913 to 53,000 in 1930.

Another development which helped to provide cheap entertainment was the growth of wireless broadcasting. The Post Office had secured authority over wireless telegraphy by an Act of 1904, and in 1922 it sponsored a company, the British Broadcasting Company, to undertake the function of broadcasting. In 1926 this company was made into a corporation with a royal charter. The advocates of private enterprise on the air were silenced by a reference to the supposedly shocking confusion existing in America. The B.B.C.'s new director-general was Sir John Reith, who had been the manager of the company since 1922. A man of strong character, he believed in instruction as well as in entertainment, and especially in

' the preservation of a high moral tone '. There was no danger of the ' bright young things ' having much influence here. The creation of the B.B.C., with its regular news bulletins, weakened the political power of the press, though it did not reduce the circulations of the national newspapers, which indulged in fierce competition. The greatest of the press barons, Lord Northcliffe, died in 1922, and only part of his empire remained in the hands of his brother, Lord Rothermere. *The Times* was bought by J. J. Astor and others, and a family trust was created for it ; and a new empire was created by the Berry brothers, based on the *Daily Sketch* and *Daily Telegraph* and a number of local papers.

The population of the country was no longer increasing at its pre-war rate. In the 1920's the national increase was only 5 per cent compared with 10 per cent in the first decade of the century. The practice of birth-control continued to spread, encouraged by the greater freedom of discussion in such matters. Because proportionately fewer children were being born, the average age of the population gradually rose. Emigration dried up after an early post-war surge—a change perhaps due in part to the development of social services. But there was a good deal of internal migration, and cities and towns continued to grow, encouraged by the improvement in transport facilities. Suburbs, served by motor-bus or electric-train services, grew up rapidly ; they were inhabited by innumerable small families of the upper working class or lower middle class, each with its small, usually semi-detached house and garden. In the case of London these developments were aided by the growth of light industry on the outskirts, and by the activity of the L.C.C. in constructing housing estates far beyond its own boundaries. Thus Hendon, Morden, Hayes, and Wembley came into existence largely as we know them now.

The extension of public transport, whether run by private or by municipal enterprise, was paralleled by an enormous growth in the ownership of motor cars and motor bicycles for personal use. The number of private cars increased more than three-fold between 1922 and 1930, when it passed the million mark ; the number of motor cycles almost doubled, to just under 700,000. There was a large number of manufacturers of motor cars, the most successful being Austin's of Birmingham, who pioneered the ' Austin Seven ' baby car, and Morris of Oxford, whose best-known models were the Morris Cowley, the Morris Oxford, and then the Morris Minor. To service these machines the countryside became disfigured by ' ribbon-building ', as it was called—garages, cafés, shops, and houses built alongside the main roads. In the large cities, and sometimes at a holiday weekend in the country, traffic jams would develop ; various plans for large-scale road improvements were made, but they were not put into operation in time to anticipate the growth in the number of vehicles. The General Strike showed that many goods customarily sent by rail could equally conveniently go by road ; and the number of commercial lorries, whether owned by professional hauliers or by business firms, increased rapidly. Civil aviation also began to develop, particularly for cross-Channel flights : in 1924 Imperial Airways was founded, and given a state subsidy to run services to the Channel Islands and Continental cities ; in the later twenties services were introduced along the route to India. In 1930 the number of passengers flown to or from Britain in British-owned aircraft was 22,045 ; in foreign-owned aircraft, 20,390.

The transport revolution, which added to the mobility of the people, had great effects on life in the country and at the seaside, for the tourist trade enormously increased, and many people went by car for holidays at the sea. It became easier for country folk to visit the towns occasionally, and retired city people were consequently more willing to reside in the country themselves if they could occasionally return to the bright lights. Agriculture, however, resumed the decline which had been temporarily reversed by the war : labourers' wages fell heavily, and their number diminished by a further quarter of a million. Arable land again went to grass ; sugar beet was subsidised, and dairy farming did tolerably well, but the wheat output was smaller than ever in 1930. Even in southern England the countryside still lacked electricity and piped water supplies.

There was a marked contrast of conditions between the areas of the staple industries, mostly in northern England, Wales, and Scotland, and the new industrial areas of London

and the south. In the former there was constant unemployment, and a tendency of the young to move south in search of
jobs. In the latter there was rapid growth, much house-
building, and comparatively little unemployment. In the
former, trade unionism was strong and ' class consciousness '
seemed most fully developed ; in the latter a new type of
suburban artisan or lower middle-class employee grew up in
which the class lines seemed to be to some extent merging.
The best avenue to advancement evidently lay through the
mushrooming service trades which catered for the products of
the new technology—electricity, automobiles, radio, chemicals,
and prepared foods. But the impact of these changes was to
be felt more in the future than at the time.

6 Depression and the Road to War, 1929-39

THE primacy of the United States in the world economy was only too well illustrated when the speculative boom on the New York stock exchange ended in sudden collapse in October 1929. The American financial distress was at once transferred to Europe, and especially to those countries in central Europe which were dependent upon American economic support. Industrial countries were already suffering from a decline in world trade, which was itself the result of the fall in world commodity prices. In Britain the number out of work rose from 1,336,000 in November 1929 to 2½ million in December 1930. In Austria and Germany the situation was even more serious, owing to the instability of their financial systems ever since the war. In May 1931 a financial crisis in Austria was precipitated by the failure of the Vienna bank, Credit Anstalt. In June and July a German financial collapse seemed imminent, and the payment of foreign liabilities was halted for six months in August. The centre of financial trouble now moved to London, where the publication of the May Committee's report on the need for governmental economy coincided with heavy withdrawals of gold to meet the European crisis. The withdrawals were made by foreign investors, who had invested in the London money market for short periods only ; their loss of confidence in the pound became marked in late July and early August. It rapidly became clear that Britain could only be maintained on the gold standard if the Bank of England could negotiate a loan of about £80 million in New York and Paris. Unfortunately for the Labour Government which was then in office, the New York bankers insisted on guarantees that the May Committee's economies would be accepted ; and to this, for political reasons, many members of the Labour Cabinet could not agree. The Labour Government fell on 24th August and MacDonald formed a new 'National' or Coalition Government to 'save the pound'.

The new Government accepted the recommended economies and secured the loan of £80 million. But the drain on gold continued, and after the 'Invergordon mutiny', when the sailors of the fleet demonstrated against cuts in their pay, it rapidly accelerated. On 19th September the Bank of England advised the Government to abandon the gold standard, which it did by hasty legislation two days later. The pound fell at once from 4·86 dollars to round about 3·40. Because this measure was undertaken by a Government supported by the Conservative and Liberal parties, it was accepted calmly in the City. It was nevertheless a revolutionary change, involving the abandonment of an international system of free financial operation. It did, however, end the drain of gold from London, and exports received a fillip from the more advantageous exchange rate.

Between 1932 and 1935 a gradual recovery of world trade took place, almost imperceptibly at first, but with gathering momentum in 1934. By 1937 it was almost back to the 1929 level, and the British share in it had slightly increased. But this was due to a rise in British imports, and not to any great revival of exports, which in 1937 were less than 85 per cent of the 1929 figure. The somewhat precarious balance of payments was improved by the decline in the value of imports owing to the continued fall in world commodity prices. In other words, the 'terms of trade', which had been moving in Britain's favour in the 1920's, became even more favourable to her, and thus many of the worst effects of the international slump were cushioned for her by the sufferings of the foreign producer. To anyone who took a long-term view of the matter, this was clearly an unhealthy state of affairs, for it could not be expected to last ; and the extent to which Britain was living on the income of her overseas investments, compared with the absence, on balance, of any fresh reinforcement to their total, was also a matter for concern.

The effects of the devaluation of the pound naturally wore off fairly soon, especially as other countries followed Britain off the gold standard, including even the United States in

1933—a move which restored the value of the pound in dollars to about 5. The 'sterling area' came into existence as Britain's immediate sphere of financial control : it consisted of the British Empire, excluding Canada and South Africa, but including a few other countries which exported heavily to Britain, such as Portugal and the three Scandinavian nations. In 1936 France also went off the gold standard, and agreed with Britain and the United States to maintain financial stability through the use of an International Exchange Equalisation Fund.

The National Government, largely dominated by Conservatives, also brought into play the remedy of Tariff Reform, which had so long been advocated as a panacea for Britain's economic difficulties. In February 1932 Neville Chamberlain as Chancellor of the Exchequer introduced a measure to give effect at long last to the proposals on which his father had staked his political future in 1903. There was to be an immediate general duty on imports of 10 per cent, with exemptions for Empire goods and certain raw materials ; further duties were to be imposed on the recommendation of an Import Duties Advisory Committee, up to a level of 33⅓ per cent. This was followed by an Imperial Economic Conference at Ottawa in the summer of 1932. The outcome of the conference fell far below the hopes of the protagonists of ' Empire Free Trade ', for the home country was anxious to protect its own farmers and also feared the loss of its export markets in foreign countries ; and the Dominions did not wish to sacrifice their own nascent industries for Britain's benefit. But a number of preferential agreements were made, and later the Colonial Empire was brought into the system, first in 1933 by the imposition of tariffs on foreign imports, and then in 1934 by the introduction of quotas for British manufactures. The result was to increase the proportion of British imports from Empire sources from 25 per cent in 1930 to 37·9 per cent in 1938 ; and the proportion of British exports to Empire countries rose from 37·5 per cent to 45·6 per cent. It was clear however that the British Empire was not likely to become a self-sufficient economic unit to the extent that Joseph Chamberlain had hoped.

These problems of economic diversity were due in part to

the Empire's already marked tendency towards decentralisation ; in part they were a cause of that tendency, which became even more marked in this period. The status of equality of the Dominions with the mother country received legal recognition by the Statute of Westminster (1931), whose preamble spoke of the ' British Commonwealth of Nations '. It was clear that in the existing state of her finances and inability to invest abroad, Britain could only seek to foster this new concept of equality and to extend it to other parts of her remaining possessions—especially the vast sub-continent of India. In 1929 the Simon Commission had reported in favour of responsible government for the provinces of India, and MacDonald sought to implement this recommendation, holding ' round table conferences ' with Indian representatives in London. After the change of Government in 1931 he held to this object, and with Baldwin's support passed the Government of India Act (1935), which was carried against strong right-wing opposition led by Churchill. India, though not yet independent, thus made a large stride in the direction of autonomy.

In view of the economic disunity of the Empire it was obvious that the only fully effective path to the recovery of world trade lay through genuinely world-wide agreements. It was unfortunate, however, that the crisis had encouraged in so many countries, including Britain, a spirit of economic nationalism. This was demonstrated in the spring of 1933 at the World Economic Conference in London, sponsored by the League of Nations, but also attended by the United States. The new American Government of Franklin Roosevelt, intent upon its own internal problems and experiments, was unwilling to support any effective measures to initiate the recovery of world trade. Consequently little was done except to introduce some international schemes for the restriction of the production of primary commodities. Henceforward relaxations of international trading barriers were largely the result of bilateral agreements between governments. Long-term international lending, like international migration, became a thing of the past, and multilateral trade seemed to be growing obsolete. Whatever the political complexions of the various governments of the world, all of them moved in the direction of a tighter control over the national economy.

Increasingly, however, attention began to be diverted to the political repercussions of the great international depression. In Germany, in particular, the depression was directly responsible for the winning of power by the National Socialist Party under Adolf Hitler in January 1933. Hitler at once proceeded to rebuild the military power of Germany, in defiance of the Treaty of Versailles, and to behave with ruthless barbarity towards his political opponents and towards the Jewish citizens of Germany, many of whom fled into exile. In October 1933 Hitler's intransigence was responsible for the break-up of the Disarmament Conference at Geneva, in spite of specific British proposals granting equality of status for Germany.

The result was that in 1934 the British Government recognised the need for rearmament, though at first little was done. Baldwin gave a pledge that the Royal Air Force would at least retain parity with all possible competitors ; and he reaffirmed Britain's ties with France by saying that the defence of England must be organised not at the Channel but on the Rhine. A Government White Paper on Rearmament was issued in March 1935, just a few days before Hitler officially announced the existence of the German air force and reintroduced conscription—both acts being breaches of the Treaty of Versailles.

In spite of these unfavourable omens, it was not easy to arouse the country to the need for military preparedness. There were several reasons for this. The traumatic effect of the First World War, with all its suffering and loss of life, made the public unwilling even to face the possibility of a similar experience. Pacifism, in the form of an opposition to all wars, however just, was not uncommon. On both Left and Right in politics there were many who felt that Germany had in fact been unjustly treated at the Treaty of Versailles, and that there was a strong case for the revision of its terms. On the Right there was sometimes a sympathy for the Nazi régime as a bulwark against Communism ; on the Left there was a belief that collective security through the League of Nations would provide a combination of force that no single power could defy. All these influences affected the Government as well as the Opposition, and independent critics such as Winston Churchill who pressed for urgency in rearmament were lone voices until it was almost too late.

Unfortunately the League of Nations, as it had evolved since 1920, was a very imperfect instrument for the prevention of war. The United States and Russia had never been members, and this fact alone is sufficient to explain its failure to take any effective measures in 1931-2 when Japan attacked Manchuria and China. After having been condemned as an aggressor Japan withdrew from the League, and Germany did likewise shortly afterwards. Although Russia became a member in 1934, it seemed to Mussolini, the dictator of Italy, that he would be running no serious risks in attacking Abyssinia, which the Italians had long coveted for their African empire. Rather to his surprise the League followed up its condemnation of his aggression, which began in October 1935, with ' sanctions ' in the form of an embargo on certain exports to Italy. But the ' sanctions ' were not sufficiently general to cripple the Italian war effort ; they did not extend to the most vital of Italy's necessities, oil ; and consequently the war ended in May 1936 with the complete occupation of Abyssinia. This was in spite of an unusual amount of support in Britain for the principle of collective security through the League, which was manifested in the ' Peace Ballot ' of the summer of 1935 when 6½ million people voted in favour of military sanctions, as against 2½ million against. Taking his cue from the Peace Ballot, Baldwin, who was now Prime Minister, fought a general election in November on a programme of support for collective security and won a handsome majority ; but it was apparent almost as soon as the election was over that the League was powerless against Mussolini. An attempt by the foreign ministers of Britain and France, Sir Samuel Hoare and Pierre Laval, to do a deal with the Italian dictator to save a fragment of independent Abyssinia was perhaps a realistic move, although under the circumstances it appeared to be highly dishonourable to the two countries and had to be disavowed.

British military and naval leaders, who found their scepticism about the League fully confirmed by events, were anxious to save Britain from the necessity of fighting both Germany and Italy simultaneously. This aim, which they expressed urgently to the political leaders, had a good deal of influence upon British foreign policy : it explains, for instance, the

Plate 11   INTER-WAR UNEMPLOYMENT.   (*Above*) A demonstration of workers in
1925.   (*Below*) A queue at a Labour Exchange.

Plate 12 POLITICS OF THE 1930's. (*Above*) British Fascists saluting Sir Oswald Mosley, 1938. (*Below*) Communists and others demonstrating against the Chamberlain Government.

otherwise extraordinary Anglo-German naval treaty of 1935, by which Britain allowed Germany to rebuild her fleet up to a maximum of 35 per cent of the British tonnage, in defiance of the Treaty of Versailles. Having made this treaty, Britain was in no position to oppose Hitler's remilitarisation of the Rhineland in March 1936. The same anxiety was at work in shaping British policy during the Spanish Civil War, which broke out in July 1936 : here, although it was clear that the rebel forces of General Franco were receiving substantial assistance from Italy and Germany, the British Government adhered to a policy of strict neutrality and turned a blind eye to the many infringements of it by the Fascist powers. Chamberlain, who succeeded Baldwin as Prime Minister early in 1937, made it his aim to secure ' appeasement ' in Europe by satisfying the immediate ambitions of both Hitler and Mussolini ; if he failed with one he hoped to succeed with the other. This policy, which subsequent knowledge has done something to justify—in reality there was little love lost between the dictators—suffered from the recognition of Anglo-French military weakness, for it was simply interpreted by the dictators as an unwillingness to resist under any circumstances. Anthony Eden, who had succeeded Hoare as Foreign Secretary, favoured a firmer policy ; but Chamberlain's insistence on courting Mussolini and snubbing Roosevelt—who had offered to take the initiative in exploring avenues to a settlement of Europe—led to Eden's resignation in February 1938.

Events then moved to a climax. In March Hitler sent his troops into Austria and incorporated that country into the Reich. Attention at once turned to Czechoslovakia, whose frontiers were now ringed by German troops, and whose population included a large German minority—the Sudeten Germans. In May a border incident led to German troop movements, but immediate representations by Britain and France prevented any sudden coup. Chamberlain determined to force Czechoslovakia—France's ally but not Britain's—to yield territory in order to satisfy Hitler's claims for the ' return ' of all Germans to the Reich. The French Government weakly accepted the British initiative ; but Hitler, for his part, had drawn up plans for the invasion of Czechoslovakia on the mistaken assumption that the Western Powers would not intervene at all.

In September, as Hitler's invasion threat became more obvious, international tension mounted, and Chamberlain decided to fly to Germany to try to come to terms with Hitler. The two leaders met at Berchtesgaden, Hitler's home in Bavaria, and then later at Godesberg on the Rhine after Chamberlain had flown home for consultations. To Chamberlain's distress the dictator kept raising his terms ; and late in September deadlock seemed inevitable. The British fleet was mobilised and air-raid precautions were put into force, with the evacuation of school-children from the industrial centres, the distribution of gas-masks, and the digging of trenches. On 28th September Chamberlain was reporting gloomily to the Commons when a sudden message from Hitler invited him to a four-power meeting at Munich, with Mussolini and Daladier, the French premier.

The Munich agreement which Chamberlain and Daladier made at the expense of the Czechs removed the immediate threat of war, and the relief which was felt in Britain took shape in a sudden adulation for Chamberlain, who returned to London claiming to have achieved, as Disraeli had done in 1878, ' peace with honour '. In fact, however, there was little honour about it : the timetable of the German invasion of Czechoslovakia proceeded almost without alteration, although without resistance ; the Germans occupied sufficient territory to deprive the Czechs of their fortifications and of all viability as an independent nation-state ; and half a million Czechs were incorporated along with the Sudeten Germans into the Reich. In return for this Chamberlain had secured from Hitler no more than a declaration of friendship for Britain. Churchill not unjustly described it as ' a total and unmitigated defeat ' ; and Duff Cooper, who was First Lord of the Admiralty, resigned from the Government in protest against the terms.

It did not take long for the Government's critics to be justified by events. In March 1939 Hitler dismembered the remaining territories of Czechoslovakia, imposing German rule on the whole of Bohemia. This step at last convinced Chamberlain that ' appeasement ' was not practicable. Rearmament in preparation for war became the country's first priority ; a Ministry of Supply was established ; and in April it was decided to introduce conscription for a period of six months' service. Chamberlain's foreign policy swung round almost to the opposite extreme : he gave unilateral guarantees of military support to distant countries which he feared were threatened by Germany or Italy—to Poland at the end of March and to Rumania and Greece in April. And he now undertook, albeit reluctantly, the task of negotiating with Russia for an alliance against Germany.

The negotiations with Russia proceeded throughout the summer, in an atmosphere of strong mutual suspicion. The full story has not yet been told ; we do not know whether the Russians ever really wished to reach agreement with the Western Powers. At all events, for much of the time the British and French Governments seemed to be dragging their feet, for they sent no prominent leader to Moscow (the British representative was Mr William Strang, a Foreign Office official), they took a long time in replying to Russian notes, and when military talks were decided on, they sent their staff delegations by sea instead of by air. On the other hand, many of the difficulties were caused by the reluctance of the small eastern European powers to admit Russian troops into their territory, even after a *casus belli* with Germany. Meanwhile the Russians had received a secret approach from the German Government, and soon they were pursuing two simultaneous negotiations. On 22nd August they announced their decision : a non-aggression pact was signed with Germany, with secret clauses for the division of eastern Europe between the two powers. It was now obvious that war between Germany and the Western Powers was imminent.

Britain had gained little militarily from the postponement effected by the Munich agreement : for although her fighting planes, the Hurricane and Spitfire, were now in production, and her new invention of radar was being widely introduced for the detection of enemy aircraft, she lost by the relative weakening of France's power *vis-à-vis* Germany, which had for some time been virtually on a war footing. The Czech army and fortifications had also been lost, and the Skoda munition works had fallen into German hands. But the

British people as a whole were aroused to the necessity of the conflict, as they had not been in 1938, and they had with them the support of the overseas Commonwealth, the governments of which all, except for that of Ireland and (at first) that of South Africa, recognised the extremity of the crisis and rallied to Britain's side.

It was in these circumstances that Hitler pressed his demands on Poland, requiring the cession of Danzig and special rights in the Polish corridor. This time he was met by firmness on the part of both his intended victim and her western allies. Early on 1st September the German invasion of Poland began ; and after a few last-minute vacillations, principally in Paris, the Western Powers declared war on Germany on 3rd September—Britain at 11 a.m., France at 5 p.m.

★

In the decade before the outbreak of war, British politics had been overshadowed by the two great international problems just discussed—the decline in world trade and the threat of military aggression from Germany, Italy, and (to a lesser extent) Japan. The first of these problems was responsible for the fall of the second Labour Government which took office in June 1929.

MacDonald's second Government was the outcome of a general election which made his party the largest in the House, with 287 seats; but it again depended on the support of 59 Liberals against 261 Conservatives, and the Cabinet again consisted largely of the more moderate leaders of the party, though this time less dependent on outside elements to complete the administration. Arthur Henderson insisted on the Foreign Office for himself, and MacDonald gave way to him, somewhat reluctantly ; Snowden was again at the Treasury ; and J. H. Thomas, the popular but unintellectual railwaymen's leader, was given special responsibility for dealing with unemployment, with the help of George Lansbury, Thomas Johnston, and Oswald Mosley. Thomas started well with a programme of grants and loans for colonial and domestic development—the Development (Loan Guarantee and Grants) Act and the Colonial Development Act, both of 1929. But almost all other plans that his group concocted were destined to wither away in the face of Snowden's grim orthodoxy at the Exchequer. In May 1930 Thomas's three assistants submitted a programme of Tariff Reform and public investment, but this was rejected by the Cabinet; Mosley resigned, to found an ill-fated little party of his own, the 'New Party'; and MacDonald took over unemployment policy himself. The result was that nothing effective was done. Snowden already had to find extra money for existing commitments, and this he did by increasing the income tax from 4s to 4s 6d and by putting up surtax rates and death duties. But he refused to budget for a deficit.

Meanwhile the Conservative Party was split once more on the question of Tariff Reform. The champions of a system of Imperial Preference were the newspaper barons, Lords Beaverbrook and Rothermere, who in 1930 joined forces to launch an 'Empire Crusade'. One of their aims was to replace Baldwin in the leadership of the party, presumably by Neville Chamberlain; and for some months they openly challenged the official party machine, putting up their own candidates at by-elections and in one or two cases getting them elected. But Baldwin fought back against what he described as ' power without responsibility—the prerogative of the harlot through the ages ', and by the middle of 1931 it became clear that the ' Empire Crusade ' was losing its force.

Thus no clear economic policy to deal with the depression was presented by either of the two major parties; and meanwhile the unemployment figures steadily increased, reaching a total of $2\frac{1}{2}$ million at the end of 1930. In February 1931 the Liberals demanded the appointment of a Committee on National Expenditure, presumably thinking the moment suitable for national economy; Snowden accepted this, and set up the Committee under the chairmanship of a business man, Sir George May. In April he introduced a budget little different from that of the previous year, but implied that further action might be necessary in the autumn. In the succeeding months the unemployment figures continued to mount.

Meanwhile the European financial crisis had developed, and it began to have a severe effect in Britain by the end of

July. The May Committee's report, recommending heavy cuts to meet an estimated budget deficit of £120 million, was published on 31st July and increased the alarm in the City. By the middle of August it was obvious that a large loan would have to be raised in New York and Paris ; but, as we have seen, the New York bankers refused to find their share unless the May Committee's recommendations were accepted by the Government. It was against this background that the Labour Cabinet met on 19th August to consider whether it could accept the list of economies amounting to a total of £78½ million, which had been proposed by government departments in line with the May Committee's recommendations.

The Cabinet deliberated for nine hours without reaching agreement. The trouble was that a large minority of its members, led by Henderson, could not accept the proposals for cuts in unemployment pay, and in this they were strongly backed by the General Council of the T.U.C., whose leaders were consulted on the 20th. The whole Cabinet did however agree to a list of economies totalling £56 million. Unfortunately for the Government, this was not enough to satisfy New York ; and on 23rd August MacDonald decided that he had no option but to resign and informed the King accordingly.

The responsibility of the monarch, as ever, was to secure the strongest possible government, and George V's action, though later much criticised, was probably the best to secure this immediate end. He discovered from Sir Herbert Samuel, the Liberal leader (in the absence of Lloyd George, who was ill), that the Liberals would favour a coalition under MacDonald ; and he learned from Baldwin that the Conservatives would be willing to accept this course as an alternative to a purely Conservative Government. The King therefore urged MacDonald to stay as Prime Minister, and to form a temporary government consisting of members of all three parties. On 24th August MacDonald accepted this commission. On his instructions the Labour Cabinet handed over their seals, and he set about constructing what was called a ' National ' administration.

It was natural that the bulk of the Labour Party, and especially the rank and file in the constituencies, should regard this as a ' betrayal ' of the movement on MacDonald's part.

He evidently hoped that the new configuration of politics would be only a passing phase, and that in a few months at the most he would be able to resume his place, if not his leadership, among his old colleagues. This was not to be. Although Snowden, Thomas, and Sankey were with him in his new Cabinet, along with four Conservatives and two Liberals, he was supported by only a handful of Labour M.P.s, and was dependent on Conservative and Liberal votes for his position in the Commons. Snowden's emergency budget, presented in September, was hotly attacked by the Labour members, and soon MacDonald and his Labour colleagues in the National Government were expelled from the Labour Party.

It was at this point that MacDonald, against Liberal advice, took the fateful step of agreeing to Conservative demands for a dissolution. The general election, which took place in October, resembled only too closely the coupon election of 1918, and MacDonald, like Lloyd George before him, won such an overwhelming success that he was entirely at the mercy of the largest component in his coalition—the Conservative Party. There were no less than 472 Conservatives in the new House ; allied with them were 33 Samuel Liberals and 35 Simon Liberals (the latter were willing to accept Tariff Reform), and 13 members of MacDonald's own ' National Labour ' group : altogether a total of 556. In opposition was the official Labour Party, which in spite of a sizeable popular vote had shrunk to the pitiful number of 46 ; there were also 5 members of the I.L.P., which had now despaired of the Labour Party ; and a family group of four independent Liberals led by the ailing Lloyd George, who well realised the dangers of MacDonald's position from his own experience.

MacDonald's new Cabinet, as reconstituted after the election, made one major change : Snowden, promoted to the House of Lords, became Lord Privy Seal and handed over the Exchequer to Neville Chamberlain. Chamberlain, in many ways a stronger man than Baldwin, naturally pressed hard for the acceptance of Tariff Reform ; but Snowden and the Samuel Liberals opposed him strongly, threatening to resign. With the new composition of the House, however, it was clear that

Chamberlain would get his way ; and in January 1932 Mac-Donald persuaded the dissentients to accept the unusual formula of ' agreement to disagree ' on this issue. The arrangement did not last long ; and in September 1932, when the Ottawa agreements were announced, Snowden and the Samuel Liberals resigned their posts. The Government now became more Conservative in complexion than ever.

Meanwhile it was obvious that other measures were necessary to secure the economic recovery of the country, and the forced abandonment of the gold standard had given Chamberlain the opportunity to encourage private enterprise with a ' cheap money ' policy. In 1932 he converted War Loan from a 5 per cent to a $3\frac{1}{2}$ per cent basis, and thus forced down interest rates. More and cheaper capital became available for the home market, especially as foreign investment was now curtailed. The result was a remarkable expansion of house-building : the annual average of houses completed rose from about 140,000 in the 1920's to over 300,000 after 1934. At the same time considerable development took place in the new industries which largely served the home market—the motor industry, road transport, electrical engineering, and rayon.

This domestic recovery was effected without any abandonment of orthodox budgetary procedures. Whereas Franklin Roosevelt in the United States was groping his way towards an expansionist policy, using a budgetary deficit to finance public works and thereby ' priming the pump ' of the national economy, Chamberlain's national accounts were as carefully balanced as Snowden's. It may well be that an acceptance of the principle of ' pump priming ', as advocated by J. M. Keynes, would have been of value in absorbing the reserve of unemployed, who remained numerous throughout the 1930's —there were still 1·3 million of them in 1937, at the peak of the recovery—but the fact remains that there was a substantial recovery in Britain which challenged comparison with the situation in any other country which had suffered from the depression. And it was effected almost entirely by private enterprise rather than by public spending.

This is not to say, however, that in Britain the world-wide phenomenon of a large increase of state regulatory powers failed to make its appearance. The powers of the Government in the control of industry, whether by encouragement or by restriction, increased rapidly, partly at least under the incentive provided by the introduction of Tariff Reform.   There were, first of all, three instances of nationalisation.   The Government took over a bill for the nationalisation of London Transport, originally introduced by Herbert Morrison as Labour Minister of Transport in 1931.   The result was the creation of the London Passenger Transport Board in 1933 to control London's tubes, buses, and trams.   The L.P.T.B. carried through an extensive programme of expansion and re-equipment in the following years.   Then in 1938 coal royalties were nationalised —a measure more important as a precedent for public owner- ship than for its own sake.   Finally, owing to the financial losses caused by competition between Imperial Airways and the new company, British Airways, it was decided in 1939 to amalgamate the two companies into a public corporation, the British Overseas Airways Corporation.

State control also manifested itself in the spread of market- ing boards for agriculture—a system initiated by the Labour Government in 1931.   The purpose of the boards was to guarantee prices which would give an incentive to the British farmer.   Where necessary, subsidies were provided by the Government : the Milk Marketing Board, for instance, was assisted by schemes to provide the distribution of cheap state- subsidised milk to mothers in the depressed areas and to school-children generally.   The sugar-beet subsidy which was inherited from the 1920's was continued, and acreage subsidies were paid for the cultivation of barley and oats.   A guaranteed price for wheat was financed by a tax on flour.   The result was a considerable increase in the amount of land under crops in the course of the decade.   The annual cost to the state of all its assistance to agriculture, which included the derating of agricultural land, was by 1939 in the neighbourhood of £100 million.

Heavy industry, which was suffering severely when the Government took office, was also helped in diverse ways, but less consistently than agriculture, although it too was much encouraged in the home market by the introduction of tariffs. The Import Duties Advisory Committee made the heavy iron and steel tariffs conditional on ' reorganisation ' in the industry, and this eventually involved the creation of an International Steel Cartel, by agreement with European producers. Little substantial change took place in the coal industry, in spite of the nationalisation of coal royalties : growth in the use of other fuels, notably oil, prevented much recovery, and unemployment remained heavy. In shipping and shipbuilding the Government intervened through the North Atlantic Shipping Act, 1934, which assisted the merger of the Cunard and White Star lines and subsidised the completion of the new giant liner, the *Queen Mary*, which was lying uncompleted on the stocks at Clydebank.

In all these ways the Government responded empirically to the demands of the times and to the pressure of the special interests involved, apparently without any particular intention of making concessions to the standpoint of the former Labour ministers in its midst. Ramsay MacDonald's personal interests lay much more in the sphere of international and imperial diplomacy, and here there was some deliberate continuity, notably in the disarmament proposals of 1933, which proved unsuccessful, and in the maintenance of the negotiations with Indian leaders, which eventually came to fruition in the Government of India Act, 1935. With this Act on the statute book—a major achievement in itself—MacDonald's last reason for staying on in a Conservative Government had disappeared ; he was growing old and tired, and his speeches had lately been characterised by a loss of precision and force. In June 1935 he exchanged offices with Baldwin, who had been in the largely honorific post of Lord President ; MacDonald retained this office until May 1937, and then retired altogether, dying in the following November. Always a moderate in domestic policy, he had great skill as a diplomat and administrator ; but his former Labour colleagues, shocked by the ' betrayal ' of 1931, failed to give him due credit for his role in the building up of their party.

It was Baldwin's misfortune that in his third and last premiership the principal difficulties arose in foreign policy, for which he cared little ; and that the need of the times was for energetic leadership, which was beyond his powers. He was, however, a shrewd electioneer by now, and by advocating a foreign policy of the type that public opinion expected—

collective security through the League, and a pledge that
' there will be no great armaments ' (a pledge only too loyally
fulfilled in the following years)—he was successful in gaining a
fresh lease of life for the National Government at the General
Election of November 1935. The Conservatives returned with
387 seats, which was still a majority of the entire House ; with
their allies, 33 Simon Liberals and 8 National Labour, they
held over two-thirds of the seats. The Labour Party recovered
to a total of 154, with many of its abler leaders such as
Morrison, Clynes, Alexander, and Dalton now returning to the
front bench. But the Samuel Liberals lost ground, being now
only 17 strong as against 26 before the dissolution. Samuel
himself was defeated, and Sir Archibald Sinclair succeeded
him as leader. Clement Attlee had already been elected leader
of the Labour Party just before the dissolution, succeeding
Lansbury whose pacifist faith was an embarrassment to a
party with a policy of collective security. Lloyd George's little
family group of 4 survived ; and there were also 4 members
of the I.L.P. and 1 Communist in the new House. The total
Government poll was just over $11\frac{1}{2}$ million, as against almost
10 million for the Opposition—a degree of balance not reflected
in the division of seats.

Almost immediately the Government aroused a storm of
hostility throughout the country as a result of the Hoare-Laval
pact for the dismemberment of Abyssinia, which was in flat
contradiction to the policy of collective security. Baldwin was
obliged to repudiate the pact and to accept the resignation of
Sir Samuel Hoare. It was fortunate for him that the election
was already over. In 1936 there was little that the Government could take credit for, in either home or foreign affairs,
until December, when an unusual crisis occurred which
brought the Prime Minister some criticism but, on the whole,
much praise. King Edward VIII, who succeeded his father,
George V, on the latter's death in January 1936, expressed the
wish to marry a Mrs Wallis Simpson, an American divorcee.
Baldwin rightly sensed that to permit the marriage would
outrage an important section of public opinion, including the
leaders of the churches. With considerable skill he presented
the King with two alternatives—abdication of the throne or
renunciation of the marriage ; and when the King preferred

to abdicate he secured the consent of all the Commonwealth governments to this unique constitutional change. (The Government of Ireland took the opportunity to remove all mention of the Crown from the Irish constitution.) Edward VIII was succeeded by his brother, the Duke of York, whose settled family life provided a favourable contrast, and who now became king as George VI.

In May 1937, basking in the reflected glory of his part in this crisis and in the public enthusiasm of a coronation month, Baldwin retired from the premiership. He left to his successor, Neville Chamberlain, an almost exclusively Conservative Government, backed by a strong majority in the Commons. But he also left him a country whose external position was gravely threatened, and whose armaments bill was running at only one-eighth of that of her most dangerous rival. Of course Chamberlain himself, as a member of the Government since 1931, was also in part responsible for this state of affairs ; but foreign policy had not previously been his special interest, and it was assumed that his determination and energy, which formed a contrast to Baldwin's listlessness, would soon transform the situation.

Unfortunately Chamberlain also had his faults, which soon became obvious as he turned his attention to these unfamiliar problems. He was narrow-minded, and tended to resent criticism, even friendly criticism, so that he was soon at loggerheads even with those who were best placed to assist him—notably Anthony Eden, the Foreign Secretary whom Baldwin had appointed to succeed Hoare. His principal adviser on foreign affairs was Sir Horace Wilson, who had made his reputation as an industrial conciliator at the Ministry of Labour ; and he was soon bypassing the Foreign Office altogether, maintaining contact with the Italian ambassador, for instance, through the medium of the head of the Conservative Central Office. It was no wonder, then, that his efforts, well meant as they were, so easily went astray.

But the political responsibility for Chamberlain's failure in 1937–9 cannot be placed entirely on his own shoulders, nor even on those of the members of Baldwin's and Chamberlain's Cabinets. The menace of German rearmament was not an official secret, and perspicacious members of all parties could have been aware of the extent of the threat in time to act strenuously to avert it.   The fact was that political leaders on all sides were unwilling to face the realities of the situation. The Labour Party tolerated Lansbury, an out-and-out pacifist, as its leader until late in 1935, and those who were concerned about the need for rearmament, such as Dalton and Bevin, took years to convince their colleagues that it was wrong to oppose the military estimates in Parliament.   Even in 1939 the Labour Party bitterly denounced the introduction of conscription.   In some ways the Liberal Party under Sinclair had a better record, but it also shared the illusions of the time. The Conservative rank and file in Parliament showed a remarkable loyalty to its official leadership, in spite of the constant campaigning of Winston Churchill and an increasing band of dissidents.   And the Conservative dissidents themselves showed great unwillingness to co-operate with other parties if it meant threatening the parliamentary position of the Government.   Although when war came it found the House almost unanimously prepared to accept the challenge, there was still no sense of unity of purpose among the parties —still less a recognition of their collective responsibility for the errors of the 1930's.

*

The severity of the depression, and the new barbarism that it gave rise to in Germany, overshadowed life in Britain in the 1930's.   It was difficult to be particularly light-hearted at a time when unemployment was soaring, or when Nazi concentration camps were being filled with Liberals, Socialists, and Jews.   A general seriousness of tone thus pervaded the second half of the inter-war period, in strong contrast to the gaiety of the 1920's.

The unemployed, it is true, were better off in Britain than in most other countries.   The ' dole ' was cut by the National Government, and the Means Test, by which those who had savings of their own or relatives able to help were deprived of benefit, was regarded as particularly unjust.   But with falling commodity prices there was not likely to be starvation, although there was plenty of hardship.   The worst feature of the life of the unemployed was its monotony and the feeling of futility that accompanied it.   In the country a man could do some gardening or poaching, and keep himself fit in various ways ; but in the towns, in spite of the efforts of various voluntary and governmental services to provide re-training or recreation, there was all too often little alternative to sheer street-corner idleness, month in and month out—often year in and year out. Some of the unemployed turned to radical politics, joining the National Unemployed Workers' Movement which was controlled by the Communist Party, and which organised demonstrations and hunger-marches to London, often culminating in angry scenes in Whitehall.   But the membership of the N.U.W.M. was surprisingly small as a proportion of the total unemployed—it had only about 40,000 adherents at the height of its influence.

The problem of unemployment would in some ways have been less serious if its incidence had been more uniform throughout the country.   It was to a large extent concentrated in those areas of Wales, Scotland, and the north of England which were dependent on staple industries of the nineteenth century—coal, textiles, and shipbuilding.   Whereas the proportion of unemployment among insured workers in London and south-east England was 13·7 per cent in 1932 and 6·4 per cent in 1937, in Wales it was 36·5 per cent in 1932 and 22·3 per cent in 1937.   At the shipbuilding town of Jarrow on the Tyne, two-thirds of the insured workers were unemployed in 1934.   The Government recognised the existence of these ' Special Areas ', as they were euphemistically called, and passed social legislation for their benefit ; but little was done to attract new industrial development to them until after 1937, when a start was made with government-subsidised trading estates.

The consequence of this regional incidence of unemployment was to encourage the younger men and women to migrate to more prosperous parts of the country, where the chances of getting employment were better.   The balance of population shifted southward : London and south-east England, with the west Midlands, gained about a million and a quarter new inhabitants between 1931 and 1938, while Wales and north-east England positively declined.   The meagreness of life in the derelict towns of the north has been well described in such works as Walter Greenwood's novel *Love on the Dole* (1933), J. B. Priestley's *English Journey* (1934), and George Orwell's *Road to Wigan Pier* (1937).

The very existence of these areas of misery and destitution acted as a powerful impetus to the intensified discussions of economic and political problems that went on in the 1930's. J. M. Keynes, who had long advocated a policy of national ' pump priming ', and who thought that Roosevelt, rather than Chamberlain, was on the right lines in economic policy, continued to exert an influence on the ideas of Lloyd George, and for that reason was somewhat suspect in Government circles. But his great contribution in this period was the carefully elaborated treatise that he addressed to his fellow-economists, the *General Theory of Unemployment, Interest and Money* (1936), which within a decade had revolutionised the whole subject of government economic policy. Keynes argued that the trade cycle could be controlled by adjustments of credit and investment, and that a government could anticipate and prevent a depression by a deliberate programme of reducing interest rates and undertaking public works, financed if necessary by a budgetary deficit.

Keynes's work was often too abstruse for the general public, but many of its implications fitted in with the trends of political discussions. It was noticed that the Russian economy, now launched on a succession of Five-Year or Four-Year Plans, appeared to be insulated from the world depression. The financial experiments of the New Deal and of Hitler's expert, Dr Schacht, also attracted attention. Many people began to feel that the second Labour Government had failed because of lack of financial expertness, and that economic planning was the key to political success. The very word ' planning ', not previously much in vogue, now had a sudden popularity. First, in 1933 there was a good deal of interest in ' technocracy ', which was an American word for the same thing ; then both Socialists and Communists began to publish books in which the idea of planning was prominent—all of them being much influenced by the Russian example. Not all the Socialists, of course, accepted the Russian pattern uncritically : the bulk of the young intellectuals who founded the New Fabian Research Bureau in 1931, and thus revived the moribund Fabian Society, did not follow their aging predecessors, Sidney and Beatrice Webb, in their fulsome praise of Soviet ' democracy '. But Communism did for the first time exercise a strong influence among professional groups —quite as much among scientists as among other intellectuals. Communist groups grew up and flourished among under-graduates at the major universities.

These developments in political thinking were accentuated by the threat of Fascism, which became very significant after Hitler's rise to power. This threat existed inside Britain as well as abroad : for Sir Oswald Mosley, who had left the Labour Party in 1930, placed himself at the head of a body called the British Union of Fascists, which with the help of Lord Rothermere and the *Daily Mail* came into some promi-nence in 1934. The B.U.F. staged a great demonstration in that year at Olympia, which was remarkable for the brutal treatment of hecklers of ' the leader '. The derivative character of the B.U.F. was only too obvious, and its anti-semitism and hostility to parliamentary institutions were not popular : it also soon lost the support of Lord Rothermere. One of the principal results of its efforts was to stimulate recruiting for the Communist Party among the Jewish population of the East End of London.

Soon, however, the threat of Fascism on the Continent assumed increasing importance, and the possibility of a new war began to loom large. This was especially so after the outbreak of the Civil War in Spain (1936–9), where Hitler and Mussolini intervened to help General Franco in his rebellion against the Republican régime. Although the major British political parties all supported non-intervention at first, left-wing sentiment in favour of the Republicans rapidly mounted. The Communist Party recruited a British battalion for the International Brigade which fought on the Republican side, suffering heavy casualties ; and the labour movement as a whole responded warmly to appeals for funds for medical supplies, food, and munitions.

The effect of this European struggle, as may be imagined, was most powerful upon the young, and especially on students at universities. For them the old party system and the anti-Communism of the leaders of the Labour Party seemed out of date and unreal. They were prepared for a ' popular front ', such as the Communists were now advocating, to unite all the opponents of Fascism, and if possible to bring Britain and France into alliance with Russia. A measure of their enthusiasm for this cause was the extraordinary success of the Left Book Club run by Victor Gollancz, which poured forth cheap editions of books in uncritical praise of the Soviet system and in bitter denigration of both Capitalism and Fascism, which were regarded as almost synonymous terms.

The relative importance of politics for the intellectuals in the 1930's can be gauged by its strong impact on one of the most personal art forms—poetry. The new poets of the decade —notably W. H. Auden, Stephen Spender, and Cecil Day Lewis—differed from their predecessors most markedly in their obsession with social problems and Socialist ideas. Some of their best work was published in the *Left Review*, a Communist-inspired publication ; and they were all much concerned in the Spanish Civil War, and went off to visit the Republican side, with varying experiences which tended to break up their unity. It must be said, however, that the Spanish War was responsible for some of the finest war poetry ever written in the English language.

Meanwhile many of the domestic social changes which had been going on in Britain since the First World War were continued in the second half of the inter-war period. Road transport, private and commercial, expanded still further, and the prevalence of road accidents caused Hore-Belisha, as Minister of Transport, to introduce various drastic reforms— a strictly enforced speed limit of 30 m.p.h. in built-up areas ; orange beacons (' Belisha beacons ') to mark pedestrian cross-ings ; official tests for new drivers. The townsman's discovery of the countryside by car went on ; but there was now also a craze, probably taken over from Germany, for ' hiking '— exploring the country on foot, camping out or staying in the inexpensive youth hostels provided by the Youth Hostels Association (founded in 1930). Keep-fit campaigns were popular ; women joined Miss Prunella Stack's League of Health and Beauty ; and a memorial fund for King George V was devoted to providing playing-fields. All this gave an impetus to the growing informality of dress for off-duty

activities.   Women could now go 'hiking' in shorts just as
men did ; and men were allowed brighter colours for sports
shirts, jackets, and even trousers.   Sun-bathing became popular, and bathing costumes for both sexes became much simpler
and briefer.   Yet women's fashionable attire was distinctly
feminine once more :   evening dresses came down to the ankle,
and lipstick and nail-varnish were widely worn.

Greater variety in recreation and entertainment was
practicable as interest increased.   Facilities for all sorts of
sports expanded rapidly :   skating at the new artificial ice-
rinks, lawn tennis in the public parks or at private clubs,
swimming in the public baths or at the seaside, swing and jazz
in the dance-halls.   Many people enjoyed their sport vicari-
ously by attending cricket and football matches or race-
meetings, or by listening to radio commentaries in their homes.
Betting on horses and greyhound races had many more addicts,
owing to the introduction of the ' Tote ' and the Irish Sweep-
stake ;   and football pools mushroomed into importance.   The
cinema was highly popular with the innovation of the ' talkies ' :
some good British films were made, notably those by Alexander
Korda ;   and a new large chain of ' Odeon ' cinemas came into
existence.   The newspapers also did a good deal to contribute
to public entertainment, largely because they were involved in
a fierce circulation war.   In 1930 the left-wing *Daily Herald*
came under the joint control of the T.U.C. and the firm of
Odham's, and began to challenge the *Daily Mail*, the *Daily
Express*, and the Liberal *News Chronicle* for the mass market.
House-to-house canvassing, prizes for crosswords and other
contests, insurance schemes and free gifts were some of the
weapons of the war—beneficial to the consumer but very
expensive to the newspapers themselves, as even the winner of
the race for circulation, the *Daily Express*, was forced to admit.
The journalists themselves also did their best, conjuring up
interest in special sensations such as the career of the Rector
of Stiffkey, who took to living in a barrel, or fresh evidence to
prove the existence of the Loch Ness Monster.   In the later
thirties it was the *Daily Mirror*, a picture paper, which under
the control of H. G. Bartholomew showed the most startling
contributions in this respect, and also the most success.   As
usual the public displayed an interest in crime, whether real

or fictitious : detective novels were highly popular, and earned large sums for skilled practitioners of the art such as Edgar Wallace, and after his death in 1932 Agatha Christie and (for a more cultured public) Dorothy Sayers.

In this serious age there was a larger market than ever before for good literature and for works which provided instruction as well as entertainment. This was shown most strikingly by the success of Penguin Books Ltd, which from 1935 issued enormous editions of good books at sixpence each. *The Listener*, a publication of the B.B.C. which printed the week's broadcast talks, also did very well ; and in 1938 an illustrated weekly concentrating on world news, *Picture Post*, was successfully launched and soon had a large sale. Books popularising science, mathematics, and even philosophy had a wide vogue ; and the B.B.C. and the gramophone companies did much to extend the appreciation of good music—the B.B.C. Symphony Orchestra was founded in 1930.

The visual arts, unfortunately, tended more and more to narrow their appeal to an audience of ' highbrows ' who were willing to encourage the boldest experimentation. Abstract painters and sculptors, who formed a group called ' Unit One ', puzzled and sometimes shocked the wider public—though not as much as the Surrealist artists who made their appearance in the middle of the decade. ' Modern ' architecture—the new style of simplicity and boldness in the use of new materials, which developed under the influence of Gropius—was also generally unpopular, though with less justification ; it had at least some notable patrons of the modern type—for instance, Boots the chemists, the *Daily Express*, and the London Passenger Transport Board.

At a time when there were more and more secular diversions, the influence of the Churches was in slow decline. Only the Roman Catholic church expanded its membership and retained a high proportion of them as church-goers. There was a certain religious revival of an unorthodox, non-sectarian kind in the so-called Oxford Group or Moral Re-armament movement, which had some success in the universities and elsewhere. But in general the proportion of church-goers was falling ; the habit of attendance no longer seemed to have status value for the middle class. An incidental result was that the Churches lost support for their attitude to such questions as divorce and Sunday amusements. The divorce law was somewhat relaxed for cases of desertion by an Act sponsored by A. P. Herbert, the independent M.P. for Oxford University, which was passed in 1937. But a sharp reminder of the influence of the Churches and their attitude to the remarriage of divorced persons was provided by the Abdication crisis.

The birth-rate, which had been falling in the 1920's, continued to decline : by 1938 the total annual number of births was less than two-thirds what it had been at the beginning of the century. Consequently the increase in the population was small, though it was larger than might have been expected owing to a net annual immigration, partly consisting of disappointed migrants to the United States and the British Dominions overseas, and partly of exiles from persecution in Germany and the countries that Germany absorbed. The drop in the birth-rate aroused some alarm at the time, and statisticians predicted that on present trends the population was likely to decrease markedly in the long run. Concern was also expressed about the health statistics, especially those of the poor, which compared unfavourably with the figures of other countries. Infantile mortality among poorer families, for instance, remained above one in ten. There were wide regional variations in the rate, which were also in part an index of poverty : in Greater London it was 51 per thousand, in Liverpool 82, in Scotland 80. But in New Zealand it was 32, in Sweden 47. Maternal mortality declined sharply in the decade, but was still at a rate double that of Holland or Scandinavia. The death-rate from tuberculosis was also falling rapidly : for England and Wales it was 1,066 per million in 1922–4, 657 in 1937 : but here again there were heavy rates in poorer parts of the country. It was clear that malnutrition, poor housing conditions, and in some areas inadequate health services prevented Britain from reaping the full benefit of progress in medical science.

In view of these facts, it is hardly true to say that Britain advanced very far in the 1930's towards eliminating the harsher inequalities of her society. Movement from one social class to another remained difficult, especially as the school-leaving age was not raised from fourteen years, and more than half the children in secondary schools were at least partly dependent on parental fee-paying. Legislation to advance the school-leaving age to fifteen lapsed at the outbreak of war in 1939. And yet a different pattern was gradually emerging in the newer industrial areas of Britain. Just as the Royal Air Force seemed to be much the most equalitarian of the fighting services, because it was the newest, its regulations permitting advancement from the ranks to an extent never secured in the Army and Navy, so in the new towns and suburbs of southern England the new working class was more comfortable and lived more like the middle class. Its daughters in cheap print frocks could look as smart as the daughters of the middle class ; its sons had greater opportunities for advancement in the new industries and trades. Although the areas of unspoilt countryside in southern England were fast diminishing as the new industrialisation went on, countless modest families found there a more generous life than they had experienced before.

7   The Second World War, 1939-45

THE war started with a German *blitzkrieg* on Poland, which brought that country to collapse within a month. The Western Allies could do little to help, especially as their military commanders were obsessed with the idea, gained from the experience of the previous war, that a defensive strategy was the best. They did not realise that the great mobility of aircraft and tanks could enable powerful offensives to be secretly mounted and quickly launched, with devastating results for an enemy who was lacking in a supply of mobile defensive strength. Unfortunately the French army was acutely short of both aircraft and tanks, and Britain could not make up the deficiency.

The first phase of the war, which lasted until the spring of 1940, was one in which little fighting took place after the defeat of the Poles. A British expeditionary force under Lord Gort took up positions in France on the left flank of the French armies, but they were not yet in contact with the enemy. The Allies' defensive strategy, coupled with Hitler's attempts to induce them to make peace while he was regrouping his forces, produced a long period of so-called ' phoney war ' in which real fighting seemed to be confined to the naval forces. A German commerce-raiding battleship, the *Admiral Graf von Spee*, was severely damaged off the River Plate and then scuttled at Montevideo ; and British naval experts showed great skill in mastering the secrets of the German magnetic mine, dropped by aircraft at the nation's estuaries. Apart from propaganda raids, the war in the air was largely limited to attacks on naval targets.

Meanwhile the Russians attacked Finland at the end of November in order to secure a strong defensive position in eastern Europe. The gallant resistance of the Finns encouraged the British and French to plan to send them assistance, if necessary forcing their way through neutral Norway ; such a move would have the incidental advantage of cutting the supply-route of Swedish iron ore to Germany. These plans had not fully matured, however, when Finnish resistance collapsed in March ; and early in April Hitler anticipated any further Allied intervention in Scandinavia by himself invading both Denmark and Norway. Denmark did not resist ; but the Norwegians fought back fiercely, sinking several German warships and transports but soon being overcome on land by the speed with which German troops secured key communication centres and landing-grounds. An Anglo-French force which landed in Norway a few days later was soon forced to withdraw owing to lack of air bases.

The failure of Allied arms in Scandinavia caused much concern in Britain, and was responsible for the fall of the Chamberlain Government and its replacement, on 10th May, by a Coalition under Winston Churchill. On the same day the Germans attacked on the western front, invading both Holland and Belgium and overwhelming their small defensive forces, and then breaking through the thinly held Ardennes, beyond the northern limit of the heavy fortifications of the Maginot line, to reach the Channel ports and to cut off the British and some of the French forces from the main French army. At the end of May it became necessary to evacuate Gort's troops and the French forces with them from the beaches of Dunkirk—an operation brilliantly carried out by the Navy with the aid of innumerable small craft from Britain and under effective air cover from bases in England. Altogether some 335,000 troops were saved, though with heavy loss of equipment.

The situation on the western front, however, was now beyond repair. After a short respite the German forces broke through the front of the remaining French forces, and on 16th June Marshal Pétain, who had taken over the French Government, asked for an armistice. The armistice terms involved the occupation by German troops of the whole of the French Atlantic coast ; and the French Government moved its capital to Vichy, in the unoccupied zone. General Charles de Gaulle, who had escaped to England, was encouraged by

SECOND WORLD WAR

/// Axis occupied territory Autumn 1942
— Vichy France and territory
···· Neutral countries

NORWAY

SWEDEN

LONDON

BERLIN
GERMANY
WARS

PARIS
FRANCE

SWITZER-
LAND

VIENNA
AUSTRIA
BU
HUN

ITALY

YUGOS

MADRID
SPAIN

ROME

Gibraltar (Br.)

Malta (Br.)

L I B

UNION OF

SOVIET SOCIALIST

REPUBLICS

Leningrad

MOSCOW

Stalingrad

Kharkov

CASPIAN SEA

A

BLACK SEA

IA

ISTANBUL

TURKEY

El Alamein

CAIRO

0   200   400   600   800 MILES

the British Government to organise ' Free French ' forces for carrying on the struggle ; and French warships at Oran and Dakar were destroyed or disabled by British naval action in order to prevent their falling into enemy hands.

Britain now had to face the immediate threat of invasion : her home defences were perilously weak, although under the inspiration of Winston Churchill her spirit was strong. Local Defence Volunteers were hastily raised to supplement the Army, but there was an acute shortage even of rifles and ammunition. The German preparations for invasion had to begin, however, with an attempt to destroy the Royal Air Force and its bases in southern England ; and the struggle to effect this—the ' Battle of Britain ' as it has justly been called —ended in failure. All through August and September German fighters and bombers swarmed across the Channel in daylight, only to meet their match in the British Spitfires and Hurricanes. Early in September the German assault was switched from the airfields to the port of London—an advantage to the R.A.F., although it resulted in heavy damage to the capital. By the beginning of October the enemy no longer dared to attack in daylight, and as the weather worsened at the end of the month it was clear that the immediate danger of invasion had passed. The ' Battle of Britain ' had been won.

The winter of 1940-1 was marked by heavy German night-bombing of British cities, especially ports, though with indifferent results from the military standpoint. The main scene of engagement for British forces now shifted to the Mediterranean and Africa, where they had to face the opposition of Italy which had declared war on both Britain and France on 10th June. Fortunately the Italian armaments were inferior to the German, and the morale of their forces was poor. The British fleet, much helped by its air arm, was able to score decisive successes against the Italian Navy at Taranto (November 1940) and Cape Matapan (March 1941). On land General Wavell's troops—British, Indian, and Australian—routed an Italian army which had advanced from Libya and drove it beyond Benghazi, with heavy loss. Italian East Africa was speedily occupied by British forces—or rather, South African and native African forces—and Abyssinia was freed. German reinforcements became essential to prevent an Italian collapse ; and in March the Italian army in Libya was stiffened by German troops under General Rommel. In April German forces invaded Yugoslavia and joined the Italians in their attack on Greece. British divisions, hastily detached from North Africa, went to Greece to stiffen the country's resistance, but they were soon driven out by the German weight, first from the mainland and then from Crete, which was captured, albeit with heavy loss, by a brilliant German paratroop operation.

It was now clear that the war was likely to engulf the whole Middle East. In April a brief campaign became necessary to oust a pro-German régime in Iraq ; and in June–July an Allied force conquered Syria and Lebanon from the Vichy French. This meant that Britain could support Turkey by land if she were invaded. But by now Hitler had already decided to concentrate on invading Russia—a decision that was ultimately fatal to his cause and which immediately relieved the pressure upon Britain both at home and in the Middle East. The German assault on Russia began on 22nd June, and secured considerable immediate success, as the Russian leaders, although warned by British Intelligence, did not expect the blow. Meanwhile German forces under Rommel remained in Libya, but they were not at first heavily reinforced, so that Wavell's successor Auchinleck was able to clear Cyrenaica again after a fierce battle at Sidi Rezegh in November.

On 7th December 1941 the Japanese entered the war with a devastating air attack, without warning, on the American fleet at Pearl Harbour. This brought the United States into the war against Germany as well ; but at first the tide of Allied reverses rose even higher. The initial surprise achieved by the Japanese enabled them rapidly to conquer the Philippines, Malaya, and British and Dutch possessions in the East Indies. The British forces in the area were handicapped by shortage of aircraft, which was largely responsible for an early disaster when two battleships, the *Prince of Wales* and *Repulse*, were sunk by Japanese air attack off the Malayan coast. Singapore, though strongly garrisoned, was obliged to surrender in February 1942. The British troops in Burma now made an arduous retreat to the Indian frontier ; and Japanese incursions into the Indian Ocean caused heavy British naval losses. Australian troops in the Middle East were hurried back to help defend their home country ; and taking advantage of the diversion of British strength, Rommel was able to capture the fortress of Tobruk and to push back the Eighth Army (as Auchinleck's main force was now called) as far as El Alamein, only seventy miles from Alexandria.

By the middle of 1942, however, the United States, recovering from the setback of Pearl Harbour six months earlier, was able to devote its huge resources to the struggle all over the world. Some American Sherman tanks were even spared for the Middle East ; and in October General Montgomery, who had taken command of the Eighth Army, won a brilliant victory at El Alamein. In the course of the following three months the Germans were forced to retire through Libya ; and meanwhile a British and American army had invaded French North Africa, under the command of the American General Eisenhower. The Germans now occupied Tunisia with fresh troops ; and the whole Allied forces in Africa, under the operational command of the British General Alexander, steadily pressed in on them and on the remnant of Rommel's original army. This campaign ended in May 1943 with a total of a quarter of a million Italian and German prisoners. Its success provided a considerable fillip to British morale, and Montgomery's skilful leadership won great praise.

Meanwhile the tide was turning in other theatres of war. The Russians had blunted the German advance in front of Moscow in 1941, and after desperate fighting in 1942 they halted a new offensive towards the Caucasus, holding the enemy at Stalingrad on the Volga and then encircling and destroying the German Sixth Army. Also in 1942, the Japanese attempt to cut off Australia from American aid was thwarted, their advances in New Guinea and the Solomon Isles being turned back after heavy fighting, including two remarkable naval actions almost entirely fought from aircraft carriers (Coral Sea and Midway).

With the turning of the tide in so many theatres of war, Churchill and Roosevelt, with the help of their Combined Chiefs of Staff—a body set up in Washington to co-ordinate

British and American strategy—could make certain vital decisions for future campaigns. They had already decided to concentrate on defeating Germany first rather than Japan—a decision partly motivated by the desire to relieve the pressure on the Russians. The Americans now sought agreement on the preparation of a joint invasion of France, although they were obliged to recognise that it could not be undertaken in the immediate future, owing to deficiencies in training and equipment. For the immediate future, British plans to attack and occupy Italy were accepted. Churchill and his advisers were great believers in the efficacy of strategic bombing, and had devoted much of Britain's strained resources to building up a Bomber Command which was steadily engaged in pounding German industrial centres—to remarkably little effect, in proportion to expense, as was discovered after the war. Personally Churchill, who in any case had prejudices against a major struggle in France, dating from the previous war, was inclined to the view that British and American bombers based on Italy as well as Britain could bring Germany to her knees. But having accepted the American proposal for an eventual invasion of France, all the British leaders turned their minds to planning the operation in the utmost detail. Much experience of the coastal defences of France was gained from commando raids, and a Combined Operations Command had already been set up to plan amphibious landings, for which special landing craft were designed.

Meanwhile one constant concern for Britain was the 'Battle of the Atlantic'—the struggle against the German U-boat menace. In this contest the Navy was hindered by not being able to use the ports of Southern Ireland, while the Germans had the advantage of the possession of bases along the whole continental coast of Europe as far south as the Spanish border. In 1941 the main area of battle was the North-West Approaches, round the north coast of Ireland. The British shortage of destroyers was considerably eased as early as September 1940 by the 'destroyer deal', by which fifty over-age American craft were transferred to Britain in return for the lease of bases in the West Indian islands. But the worst phase of the battle came only in 1942, when America had entered the war, for the United States Navy was incapable of coping effectively with the submarines in American waters. Convoys bound for Russia by the northern route and for Malta through the Mediterranean also suffered heavily from air attack as well as from submarines. This gave added weight to the arguments in favour of freeing the Mediterranean before attempting to cross the Channel in force.

In July 1943 an Allied army under General Alexander invaded Sicily, and soon swept it clear of the enemy. These events led to a crisis in Italian politics ; by the beginning of September Mussolini had been deposed and a new Italian Government made an armistice with the Allies. The invasion of Italy was therefore initiated at once, and two Allied armies under General Alexander forced their way up the peninsula, only to find that strong German forces were facing them, fighting with determination and taking full advantage of the difficult terrain. In February 1944 a bold attempt was made to speed up the campaign by a landing at Anzio, behind the German lines ; but the going remained difficult, and Rome did not fall until 4th June. Meanwhile the Russians had gradually established their superiority over the German armies in the east, and had pressed them back to a line roughly corresponding to the pre-war Russian frontier.

On 6th June 1944 the expected invasion of northern France began. General Eisenhower was in supreme command, but General Montgomery was the operational commander of all troops until 1st September. His plan was to seize the Normandy coast and, while British troops on the left flank were to hold enemy reinforcements from the east, American armoured forces were to break out southwards from the right flank. This plan worked : the American forces wheeled east and cut off a number of German divisions at Falaise. By the end of August the Germans were in full flight from France, the more so as fresh landings by American and Free French forces had taken place near Cannes. The whole operation was a model of careful planning and vigorous execution, under the bold and confident tactical control of Montgomery, now a very experienced army commander.

On 3rd September British troops entered Brussels ; next day Antwerp was taken. In the hope of ending the war at a single blow, Montgomery urged Eisenhower to make a single powerful thrust towards the Ruhr. Eisenhower, however, favoured a broad-front strategy by all the Allied armies. At the same time he did allow Montgomery to employ the whole reserve of air-borne troops. These forces were landed at Nijmegen and Arnhem in Holland, with the object of securing a crossing of the Rhine. The Arnhem position however was just beyond the powers of the land forces to reach and to relieve, owing to their extended communications. It became clear that the war would drag on through the winter ; and the Canadian First Army had some difficulty in clearing the Scheldt estuary, including the island of Walcheren, so that the port of Antwerp could be used. By this time the Allied forces, including a vast build-up of American troops, had closed up to the German frontier ; and the Russians had entered East Prussia and invested Budapest. British troops also moved into Greece, where towards the end of 1944 they found themselves fighting to suppress a left-wing insurrection against the old régime.

Roosevelt, Stalin, and Churchill met at Yalta in the Crimea early in February 1945 to make final plans for the immediate post-war occupation of Europe ; and the final Western offensive of the war against Germany began in the same month. While American armies pushed into the Rhineland in the south, Montgomery's 21st Army Group (Canadian First Army, British Second Army, and American Ninth Army) cleared the northern Rhineland and then in March forced a crossing of the Rhine, again with the help of air-borne troops. With constant pressure being exerted on all fronts, the enemy's resistance collapsed. By 25th April the Russians had sur-rounded Berlin, and the Allied armies in Italy had crossed the Po. On 2nd May the German troops on the Italian Front surrendered ; on 4th May Montgomery received the surrender of the forces in north-west Germany, Holland, and Denmark ; and on the 7th, Hitler having committed suicide in Berlin, Doenitz, whom he had appointed to succeed him, capitulated to Eisenhower.

There has been considerable controversy about the relative merits of the Allied army commanders. In particular, Mont-gomery has criticised Eisenhower for his broad-front strategy, which he believes was responsible for prolonging the war.

Eisenhower, however, had to take political considerations into account, and as Supreme Commander he deserves high praise for his skill and tact in welding the Allied staffs into a common team. No comparable success was achieved in the First World War.

Meanwhile Lord Louis Mountbatten, responsible for the South-East Asia Command, had been planning warfare against the Japanese ; and in Burma the British Fourteenth Army under General Slim, with a good deal of American supply help, had been fighting a difficult jungle campaign against the Japanese. At the end of 1944 Slim was able to take the offensive, and in the following months he cleared Burma, capturing Rangoon on 3rd May. Preparations had been made for an invasion of Malaya when on 10th August the Japanese capitulated, having been soundly defeated in naval and air warfare in the Pacific which culminated in heavy raids on the home islands and in the dropping of the first two atomic bombs at Hiroshima and Nagasaki. The natural elation that people felt at the end of the war was numbed by horror at the devastation caused by these new weapons.

Total British casualties in the war were substantially less than in the First World War, although they were slightly more than the United States total. The armed forces lost 303,000 killed, and to this must be added a further 109,000 for the remainder of the Commonwealth and Empire. In addition more than 60,000 civilians were killed in air raids, and some 30,000 members of the Merchant Navy lost their lives. The Russian dead, it may be noted, amounted to over twelve million, including at least five million civilians.

*

At the outbreak of war in 1939 Chamberlain had been anxious to broaden the basis of his Government. He brought in Churchill as First Lord of the Admiralty and Eden as Dominions Secretary, and also called upon two distinguished public servants, Lord Chatfield and Lord Hankey, to be Minister for the Co-ordination of Defence and Minister without Portfolio respectively. A War Cabinet of nine was constituted, of which as Churchill pointed out the average age was 64—

Plate 13 PRELUDE TO MUNICH. Neville Chamberlain leaving for Munich, 29 September 1938. Behind, right : Leslie Hore-Belisha.

Plate 14 THE SECOND WORLD WAR. (*Above*) Mr and Mrs Winston Churchill surveying bomb damage in London, 1940. (*Below*) A British tank (an American Sherman) moving forward in France, 1944.

' only one year short of the Old Age Pension ! ' Churchill himself was just at this average age. Meanwhile the Labour and Liberal parties refused all suggestion of a coalition under Chamberlain, although they agreed to an electoral truce. They bided their time, regarding the new Government as on probation.

The Norwegian campaign, with its revelation of Allied weakness in air power, brought the period of probation to an abrupt end. Chamberlain had just previously been indulging in foolish optimism, saying early in April that Hitler had ' missed the bus '. In the debate on the Norwegian campaign, not all Churchill's store of oratory could outweigh the effect of criticism from Conservative backbenchers, including the veteran L. S. Amery, who quoted Cromwell's words to the Long Parliament, ending ' In the name of God, go ! ' The Labour vote of censure was supported by some 40 Conservatives, and many more abstained, so that the Government majority fell to 81 (281–200).

Under these circumstances Chamberlain tried at first to form a Coalition Government, but in the face of Labour hostility he was reluctantly obliged to resign in favour of Churchill, whom the Labour Party was prepared to accept as Prime Minister. On 10th May, just as Hitler's western offensive began, Churchill took office and formed a small War Cabinet with Halifax, Chamberlain, and the two Labour leaders, Attlee and Arthur Greenwood. Churchill kept for himself the Ministry of Defence, and thus exercised a general supervision of the fighting forces ; Halifax remained as Foreign Secretary ; and the others for the time being were given no major administrative duties. Among other appointments were Beaverbrook as Minister of Aircraft Production, which now assumed the highest priority ; Ernest Bevin, brought in from his trade union office to serve as Minister of Labour and National Service ; Amery as Secretary for India ; and the Liberal leader Sir Archibald Sinclair as Air Minister. Beaverbrook was brought into the War Cabinet in August, Bevin in September.

The months of crisis in the summer and autumn of 1940 brought out the matchless quality of Churchill's leadership. His speeches breathed determination and energy, and it was evident that he enjoyed his responsibilities in spite of their weight.   As he himself said, ' I readily admit that the part which had now fallen to me was the one I liked the best.'   He was no longer in the invidious situation that he had held in the First World War, of seeing his ideas fail for lack of support from his colleagues ; he was not even in the position of the Prime Minister of that war, Lloyd George, whose authority hardly extended to the battlefields.   Churchill now had great military prestige, based on his long experience of war both as combatant and as minister and on his prescience about the course of German rearmament.   In Parliament he had no formal opposition to meet, and the post of Leader of the Opposition went into abeyance.   The medium of broadcasting, which enabled the people as a whole to sense his quality of leadership, had also reduced the power of the newspapers to make or unmake a national figure.   Finally, in September 1940 Chamberlain, who was still leader of the Conservative Party, was obliged to retire from politics owing to ill health, and Churchill was elected to the vacant party leadership.

In the War Cabinet the balance of the parties had to be roughly maintained, and Churchill managed to do this and at the same time improve its administrative capacity.   Chamberlain he replaced by Sir John Anderson, an outstanding product of the Civil Service, whom Churchill jocularly described to Attlee as ' the automatic pilot '.   Halifax he shortly sent as ambassador to the United States, replacing him as Foreign Secretary by the more energetic Eden.   Such was the team for 1941.   In the following year the ailing Beaverbrook was replaced by Oliver Lyttelton, who became Minister of Production, and Arthur Greenwood was replaced for a time by Sir Stafford Cripps, the Socialist lawyer, and then later by Herbert Morrison.   Sir John Anderson continued to be the real power on the home front, his ' Lord President's Committee ' being the steering authority of a number of Cabinet committees dealing with home policy. Anderson took over the Exchequer in 1943 when Sir Kingsley Wood died, but he retained many of his earlier duties as well.

Naturally parliamentary criticism was strongest at times of military adversity.   The most serious challenge to the Government came just after the fall of Tobruk in June 1942.   A vote of censure was then moved by Sir John Wardlaw Milne, the

Conservative Chairman of the Commons Finance Committee, and supported by Admiral Sir Roger Keyes and by Leslie Hore-Belisha, who had served as Secretary for War. But the critics were not united in their ideas, and no constructive alternative to the existing Government's policy emerged in the debates. The vote of censure secured only 25 supporters ; and the turning tide of war in the following months silenced further criticism.

This did not, however, give Churchill as free a hand in the determination of subsequent strategy as he would have liked. From 1942 onwards his plans had to be more and more carefully co-ordinated with those of the Americans, and he had to recognise that the Americans were in fact the senior partners in the joint planning, for their effort soon became the larger. It was also necessary to keep in touch with the Russians, though geography largely prevented joint operations with them, and various other difficulties, mostly political in origin, prevented really friendly relations. All these responsibilities kept Churchill busy travelling the world, and he could not devote as much time as a Prime Minister would normally give to the country's domestic problems.

On the whole, however, the balance of domestic legislation and administration was fairly well kept between the Conservative and Labour points of view. The Labour Party was not as well represented in Parliament as the state of public opinion would have justified ; but on many issues they received support from a ' Tory reform ' group which had developed among their erstwhile opponents. There was always in any case a substantial ministerial vote in the House to tide over crises, as well as a considerable reluctance on the part of Members to embarrass the Government. Two critical votes of 1943 illustrate this. Although many Conservatives were dissatisfied with Ernest Bevin's Catering Bill for the state regulation of wages in the industry, its second reading passed by 283 votes to 116 ; and in spite of acute Labour disappointment, the Government's cautious approach to the question of social security was approved by 335 to 119. In the same year Herbert Morrison, the Labour Minister for Home Security, braved the wrath of his own followers by releasing the Fascist leader, Sir Oswald Mosley, from detention.

Inevitably the Government had to shape policies to deal with the problems of post-war reconstruction. In a highly planned economy such as Britain's had become, these things could not be left to chance, and the acres of desolation in London and other cities as a result of air raids were a constant reminder of the need for rebuilding. A number of official committees had been set up to consider some of the most important problems of reconstruction, and their reports helped to focus the issues involved. The Scott report of 1942 recommended effective state control of rural development ; and the Uthwatt report of the same year urged a form of nationalisation of land values and ministerial control of the siting of new construction. As a result a Town and Country Planning Act was passed in 1944 to increase the compulsory powers of the local and central government in this sphere. Further, the Barlow report of 1940, which proposed a planned allocation of new industrial development to the old distressed areas, was taken up by Hugh Dalton as President of the Board of Trade and led to his Location of Industry Act, finally passed in 1945 just after the end of the Coalition. Keynes's influence as wartime adviser at the Treasury led to the 1944 White Paper on Employment Policy, which pledged the Government to a deliberate policy of securing full employment by financial measures—a development which signalised a revolution in economic thought. In the same year the Minister of Education, R. A. Butler, piloted through the House an Education Bill which provided for the raising of the school-leaving age to fifteen and for part-time education up to the age of eighteen.

The issue that caused the greatest controversy, however, was that of social security. In December 1942 Sir William Beveridge, who as a Civil Servant had played an important part in shaping the social reforms of the Asquith Government, presented the findings of a study that he had made for further improvements in the existing services. He advocated their unification into a single system covering the whole population and all types of need. He proposed the establishment of a free National Health Scheme, and the enlargement and extension of existing financial benefits, including the introduction of children's allowances. The whole field, he thought, should be the responsibility of a new ministry, a Ministry of

Social Security. Beveridge's ideas were too sweeping for the Coalition as a whole to accept without much deliberation, but the Labour Party at once embraced them enthusiastically. Public opinion was keenly interested in the proposals, and seemed to look for some sort of commitment from the Government. Churchill was not anxious to have a controversy on a domestic question of this importance while the war was yet far from won ; but he did appoint a Minister of Reconstruction—Lord Woolton, an able business man who while inclined to be conservative was not a Conservative politician, and who had made a name for himself in the course of the war as Minister of Food. In 1944 Woolton produced a White Paper on Social Insurance which accepted many of Beveridge's ideas, but not all ; and in 1945 a Family Allowances Act was passed to implement one important recommendation.

These measures went some way, but evidently not far enough, to satisfy the ever-growing radicalism of public opinion. It was clear that the success of the planned economy, as exemplified both in wartime Britain and also in Soviet Russia, had made a great impression generally ; and in spite of the electoral truce it was becoming impossible to prevent controversy on these issues at by-elections. Sir Richard Acland, who had been elected as a Liberal, founded a Commonwealth Party which was Socialist in tone ; this body intervened at a number of contests and secured substantial votes. In January 1944 two almost simultaneous by-elections resulted in victories for left-wing independents. The opening of the battle in Normandy stilled this rising political activity, but it was a portent of the future.

In the spring of 1945, when it became clear that the war with Germany was almost won, there began to be talk of an early election. It was generally thought that this would favour the Conservatives, owing to the immense reputation that their leader Churchill would have as the architect of victory. Churchill himself took this view, and he decided to offer the Labour Party the alternative of an immediate election or a continuation of the Coalition until the Japanese surrender, when again his reputation would probably be at a peak. Attlee replied that his party would continue the Coalition until October, but no further. Churchill thereupon decided on an immediate dissolution. On 25th May the Coalition came to an end, and Churchill formed a ' caretaker ' Government consisting of Conservatives and those who were willing to serve as their allies—the old Simon Liberals among them. The election was fixed for 5th July, but owing to the delay involved in bringing in the postal vote from the armed forces abroad the count was not to be until 26th July.

The Labour Party's electoral machine was on the whole in better shape than that of the Conservatives, for many of its voluntary workers had remained at home in reserved occupations. But it had other advantages : its election manifesto, *Let Us Face the Future*, was a model of simple and clear explanation of a limited programme of nationalisation and a planned transition to a peacetime economy with the retention of government controls as a safeguard ' against the chaos which would follow the end of all public control '. The Conservative programme was much less definite : ' We should examine the conditions and the vital needs of every industry on its own merits.'

The election was naturally a quiet one. The leaders had some difficulty in abusing each other after having been colleagues for so long. Churchill invited Attlee to accompany him to a conference with President Truman (Roosevelt's successor) and Stalin at Potsdam in June, and the nearest thing to an election sensation arose out of this. Professor Laski, the chairman of the Labour Party executive, issued a statement saying that Attlee could not commit the Labour Party to the Potsdam decisions ; and Churchill saw an opportunity of exploiting this remark (which Attlee at once repudiated) in order to suggest that the parliamentary Labour leaders were not their own masters. In a B.B.C. broadcast he also suggested that the Socialist programme of the Labour Party would necessitate ' some form of Gestapo, no doubt very humanely directed in the first instance '. These attacks, which were thought by the Labour leaders to have been instigated by Lord Beaverbrook, caused Attlee to retort, ' I object to this country being ruled from Fleet Street, however big the circulation, instead of from Parliament.'

These exchanges did not seem to make much impact on the electorate : its concern was probably more with the

character of the transition from war to peace, and with the
need to avoid the difficulties that followed demobilisation in
1918. As usual, the voters showed more signs of reacting
against an unpleasant experience in the past than of deliberately embracing a doctrinaire programme for the future.
They were determined to throw out the pre-war majority, the
' men of Munich ' ; but they were not really registering an
endorsement for Socialism. All the same, the election resulted
in a very large number of Socialists being returned to Parliament, just as in 1906 the social reformers of the Liberal Party
had benefited from the reaction against Joseph Chamberlain's
fiscal proposals. The new Commons would contain 393 members of the Labour Party—an ample majority of the whole
House. The Conservatives and their allies were reduced to
213 ; and there were 12 Liberals, 3 I.L.P., 2 Communists, and
2 Irish Nationalists as well as 14 Independents. Churchill
immediately resigned office, and Attlee became Prime Minister,
to form the first Labour Government with a Commons majority.
Churchill's great prestige had not been enough to overcome
the hostility to his party which had developed over the years
when he himself was out of office ; and so the great war
leader was rejected at the polls at the very moment that his
achievements were being acclaimed by the world at large.

★

The years of tension before the war, if they had not produced an adequate level of armaments, had at least enabled
the Government to prepare plans for the nation's mobilisation
on the home front ; and it would be true to say that the bulk
of economic and social change during the war, where it was
not the result of direct enemy action, was the product of
conscious administrative policy. Most of the leading Civil
Servants and politicians had some experience of the domestic
problems of the First World War, and they laid their plans so
as to achieve as soon as possible the degree of control already
attained by 1918. September 1939 therefore saw some
immediate developments in this direction : the assumption of
wide powers by the Government ; the establishment of
Ministries of Economic Warfare, Information, Food, and

Shipping ; and also national registration and the issuing of identity cards to the entire population. In anticipation of heavy air raids, children were evacuated into the country from London and other industrial centres ; and the air-raid precautions system was at once put on the alert. Heavy taxation was introduced in the expectation of a war of at least three years' duration : in order to prevent an immediate inflation, the income tax was raised to 7s 6d in the pound and a heavy Excess Profits Tax was introduced.

Inevitably, however, the absence of any large-scale fighting before April 1940 deprived the nation as a whole of a full sense of wartime urgency. Children began to drift back from their billets in the country when no air raids took place ; and many people found to their surprise that their wartime lives at first differed little from their normal peacetime existence— except that the carrying of gas-masks in cardboard boxes and the observance of a complete black-out at night were universal. The call-up of age-groups for service with the armed forces proceeded much more systematically than in the First World War, but had not got beyond the 25-year-olds by April 1940 ; and until that month there still remained a reserve of unemployed amounting to over a million. Rationing began only in January, and was at first restricted to sugar, butter, and bacon.

The events of the spring and summer abruptly ended this period of ' twilight ' war. The invasion of Britain itself suddenly became an immediate probability. Hasty measures were taken to intern Fascists and enemy aliens, for fear that they might organise a ' Fifth Column ' of enemy sympathisers ; and the detainees were only gradually sorted out into the friendly and the hostile. Local Defence Volunteers—later known as the ' Home Guard '—were quickly raised to help the regular forces to resist an invasion ; and defences were improvised throughout the country—mines on the beaches, poles on possible landing-grounds, concrete pillboxes, barbed wire, and anti-tank obstacles on all proposed lines of defence. Camouflage paint appeared everywhere, and signposts disappeared from the roads. The success of the Royal Air Force in the Battle of Britain was of course a great fillip to national morale ; but the invasion was still hourly expected, and everywhere men stood by with all sorts of weapons—shotguns and even pikes to supplement the shortage of rifles—ready to grapple with the enemy as soon as the church bells rang out (for this was to be the signal).

As the weather worsened in October, it became clear that the invasion was at least postponed until 1941. The main concern of the people was now with the heavy night air raids. The local fire-brigades were doing their best to cope with incendiary attacks, supplemented by the Auxiliary Fire Service ; but very extensive damage was done late in the year—especially in Coventry and in the City of London—until two important measures were taken : the fire services were amalgamated into a National Fire Service, under the Ministry of Home Security ; and a service of fire-watchers, armed with stirrup-pumps and buckets of sand, was organised to watch for incendiary bombs. This put an end to the incendiary threat. But there were also heavy casualties from high-explosive bombs and mines, and many people were bombed out of their homes in the larger cities. In London the number of air-raid shelters was inadequate, and the people insisted on occupying the platforms of the ' tubes ' : in due course this was accepted, and emergency arrangements were made to make the tubes habitable and to provide other deep shelters. People in the suburbs were more usually content to rely on the ' Anderson ' shelter in the garden, or the stronger ' Morrison ' shelter that was later devised by the Government and issued in large numbers where most needed. The damage to the cities went on, however, for neither anti-aircraft artillery nor night fighters—the two main methods of defence—were very efficient at first. On the night of 10th May 1941 the Chamber of the House of Commons was destroyed by a bomb, and the Members had later to accept the hospitality of the House of Lords. Shortly afterwards, however, the raids became much less intensive owing to the diversion of German air strength to the eastern front, which opened with the invasion of Russia in June.

At first the industrial war effort was limited by the need to continue making goods for export, so as to pay for some at least of the raw materials and equipment bought in the United States and elsewhere. Only in March 1941 was the system of ' cash and carry ' for purchases from America replaced by the generous 'lend-lease' programme, which was the clearest possible earnest of American sympathy with the British cause. But the complexity of the equipment required for the forces——and especially for the R.A.F.—meant that a high proportion of the available skilled labour had to be kept in the factories. In 1941 a ceiling of 'about two million' was placed upon the total number of men in the Army; and even this figure could not be maintained without the strictest control of manpower, involving (at the end of 1941) the direction of men over military age and of women as well into jobs of national importance. By this time there were already over 200,000 women in the auxiliary sections of the armed forces, nearly half of them in the Army's Auxiliary Territorial Service. By the end of the war these numbers had almost doubled, and women were even serving in anti-aircraft teams. Many were also working on the land in the Women's Land Army.

In the factories there was comparatively little unrest in spite of the severe dislocation of production often caused by bombing. This was because of the loyal support of the war effort given by the labour movement, and the authority given to its parliamentary representatives to deal administratively, under the Coalition Government, with problems affecting the workers. Herbert Morrison, the Minister of Home Security, had been the leader of the L.C.C. Labour majority; and Ernest Bevin, the Minister of Labour, had been secretary of the largest of the unions, the Transport and General. Bevin's Essential Works Order, which provided for the direction of labour, sugared the pill by laying an obligation on employers to provide for the welfare of their workers; and a remarkable development of welfare services did take place—factory canteens, nursery schools for the children of women workers, 'music while you work', and so on. After the German invasion of Russia, even the Communists, who had previously encouraged discontent in the factories, became keen supporters of the production drive, in the knowledge that some of the output was being shipped to the Red Army.

By 1942 the country's economy was in a fully mobilised state, and there was very little 'slack' that could still be taken up. Production for consumers' needs had been cut down to the essential minimum by the purchase tax, by a quota scheme for allocating materials to manufacturers, and by a system of establishing 'utility' standards. With the introduction of 'points' at the end of 1941 a very wide extent of food rationing was in existence ; clothing rationing also began in 1941. Fuel was not rationed, but consumption was much reduced by voluntary economy, and in 1942 a new Ministry was established to supervise the supply and to take control of the coal industry. Later in the war it became necessary to direct into mining a proportion of the young men who became available for national service—the 'Bevin Boys' as they were called.

In 1943 and early 1944 the preparations for the invasion of Europe were being made, and American help in the supply of munitions and equipment enabled the Government to increase the size of the armed forces at the expense of industry. By early 1945 the Commonwealth forces were getting only two-thirds of their supplies from the United Kingdom : 10 per cent came from Canada and over 20 per cent from the United States, under the lend-lease programme. There were, of course, many supplies provided by Britain to her allies under similar arrangements ; this was especially the case when American forces came to Britain in large numbers and required local supplies and facilities. In addition both Britain and America were sending much help to Russia ; and Britain had since 1940 built up the military forces of the Free French, and of the Poles and other national groups in exile from occupied Europe. But the assistance of America outweighed all this and, as Churchill said, it enabled Britain, a nation of forty-eight million, to fight as if she were a nation of fifty-eight million. This support the Americans were able to provide without ever mobilising their resources of manpower to anywhere near the limit ; such was their power. Britain, if not so strong, could at least be proud that her effort was complete : in June 1944, out of every nine members of the potential labour force in the country, two were in the armed forces and three engaged on war production. No other country ever quite equalled this proportion, but it was maintained by Britain at almost the same level for three years. The fact that manpower budgeting became the most important sphere of domestic policy in Britain after 1941 was clear evidence of the country's complete mobilisation.

The country also had much cause for satisfaction with the effective use made of its scientific resources. The Department of Scientific and Industrial Research, which was founded in the First World War, was able to direct, at least in their initial stages, a number of projects of vital importance for the war effort. Among these were work on radiolocation of enemy aircraft, or radar as it was called ; investigation of the properties of explosives and the devising of serviceable flame-throwers ; and some initial work on the problems of the atomic bomb (which owed much to research at Cambridge carried out before the war by Rutherford, Cockcroft, and others). The latter undertaking was given high priority in 1941, under the code name of ' Tube Alloys Research ', but the manufacture of the bomb was finally undertaken, with British scientific help, in the United States and Canada.

Of course the armed forces also had their experimental teams of scientists. The Royal Aircraft Establishment at Farnborough was responsible for work on Whittle's jet engine, which resulted in vast increases in aircraft speeds at the end of the war. The Germans, it must be said, were abreast of this work ; and Hitler's ' secret weapons ', the pilotless bomb or ' V1 ' which was used from sites in France in the summer of 1944, and the rocket or ' V2 ' which was used from Holland in the autumn of the same year, were both achievements of major importance which might have been decisive if they had come earlier, or been just a little more efficient in performance. Air photography and its interpretation made great strides, and enabled the R.A.F. to devise counter-measures to foil the enemy's plans. British medical research was also responsible for a very important advance by the discovery of penicillin, which was of value for a range of conditions extending to more than half the possible total of cases requiring emergency treatment. As with the military application of atomic energy, work carried out with great success in British laboratories was put to productive use in the United States, where resources were more readily available.

Meanwhile the arts remained vigorously alive, and were even stimulated by the siege conditions of war time. Public money supported a Council for the Encouragement of Music and the Arts ; and the Ministry of Information financed documentary films which were often of considerable artistic merit. David Lean and Noel Coward successfully exploited a patriotic theme with *This Happy Breed* and *In Which We Serve*. The Old Vic, bombed out from the Waterloo Road, moved to the New Theatre and with Laurence Olivier and Ralph Richardson achieved an unusually high standard of excellence. The air raids and the damage they caused provided inspiration for several artists, notably Henry Moore, Graham Sutherland, Paul Nash, and John Piper. Writers, too, responded to the challenge—Stephen Spender, Henry Green, and William Sansom among others. George Orwell and J. B. Priestley produced powerful interpretations of the popular mood in wartime Britain—interpretations that sometimes proved controversial, as Priestley found with his broadcast ' postscripts '. Cyril Connolly's *Horizon* and John Lehmann's *New Writing* were periodicals which provided vehicles for the best wartime literature, some of it ephemeral but some of it of real quality, and all very widely read. A few very good young poets emerged—two of the best, Sidney Keyes and Alun Lewis, being killed in action. The audience for good music continued to increase, and lunchtime concerts were much appreciated by office workers and servicemen on leave.

These cultural achievements in wartime reflected a degree of collective solidarity which the country had rarely attained before. Artists and people shared a common experience, and the artists, in interpreting it, reached a wider audience than usual. This was all to the good : and many people hoped that it could be continued after the war. The problems of post-war reconstruction, as we have seen, aroused wide attention from 1942 onwards, and the Government itself provided a stimulus to discussions on the subject by requiring time to be set aside in training the troops for lectures on current affairs. Certain issues such as the Beveridge Report proved somewhat embarrassing—a pamphlet on this question by the Army Bureau of Current Affairs had to be withdrawn because it was too friendly to the report. But by 1943 and 1944 there was no doubt that a new tide of radicalism was rising both in the forces and in the factories. Thus it was that a new Britain seemed to come thrusting through the ruins of the old.

8 Reconstruction, 1945-55

BRITAIN entered the post-war world with many of the same economic difficulties that had embarrassed her between the wars in her relations with the rest of the world—but now decidedly increased by her six years of military effort. The sale of British investments overseas, which had proceeded rapidly in the early years of the war, had been largely halted by the freedom of supplies under lend-lease, but the process had not been reversed ; and the abrupt termination of lend-lease on 2nd September 1945, almost immediately after the Japanese surrender, brought the new Labour Government at once into a grave financial crisis. External liabilities had in fact increased by nearly £3,000 million, of which one-third had been met by the sale of external investments. There were other causes for concern about the future : in the course of the war the country had lost eighteen million tons of shipping, only about two-thirds of which had been made up by new building. About five million houses in Britain had been destroyed or damaged, and a great deal of the country's industry was sadly behindhand in the state of its capital equipment.

To meet this situation Keynes was dispatched by the new Government to negotiate a new loan of $3,750 million from the United States. It was hoped that this would tide Britain over a transitional period, in the course of which her export industries would be redeveloped sufficiently to enable her to pay her way. It had been calculated that if exports could be raised to 175 per cent of the pre-war level, the country could bring its finances into balance once more. Unfortunately, however, the immediate post-war period saw an unexpected worsening of the terms of trade, owing to the shortage and hence expensiveness of various raw materials. Consequently an increase in exports of 75 per cent was an inadequate target ; and in the meantime the money from the loan, which was being used for raw material imports, ran out more rapidly than was expected.

The loan agreement also imposed upon Britain the obligation to restore the convertibility of sterling at an early date. It was this obligation, fulfilled in 1947, which precipitated a financial crisis and brought the nation face to face with its external difficulties. Convertibility had to be abandoned, and harsh measures of domestic restriction were undertaken by Sir Stafford Cripps, the Chancellor of the Exchequer, in order to cut down dollar imports and so restore the situation for the time being. Very fortunately for Britain, the American Government now undertook to provide large-scale financial assistance for the recovery of Europe under the so-called ' Marshall Plan '. This liberal decision was prompted by the fear that Europe might fail to rebuild its economic strength, and that Communism would make rapid gains as a result. Accordingly an Organisation for European Economic Co-operation (O.E.E.C.) was set up, to provide dollar aid for the European nations and to encourage them to work together by joint economic planning and the removal of mutual tariff barriers.

The American aim was to build up a viable European economy by establishing a free-trade or freer-trade area comparable with the internal market of the United States. This enlightened plan did not take sufficient account of the political difficulties involved in integrating the European countries. The British economy in particular, linked as it was with the Commonwealth countries and the almost co-terminous sterling area, was not readily assimilable to those of the Continental countries. But Britain benefited considerably from the dollar assistance provided in the years between 1947 and 1950, and thereafter she was able to manage without American aid once more, largely owing to unexpectedly large raw-material shipments from British colonies to the United States.

With or without direct dollar assistance, Britain was now extremely dependent on the United States, and changes of American domestic economic policy even if comparatively small could have an immediate and serious effect on the

situation in Britain.   Thus in 1949 a slight recession in the
United States which reduced the volume of imports from the
sterling area was enough—in spite of Marshall Aid—to force
Cripps to devalue the pound (from $4·03 to $2·80).   Then
again in 1951, when American stockpiling of raw materials
from British colonies ceased, a fresh financial crisis took place
in Britain and led to a renewal of efforts to cut down on dollar
imports.   British Governments, irrespective of political complexion, had to retain careful control of the country's foreign
exchange situation, and were obliged to limit the use of foreign
currency by British tourists, making travel for pleasure in
America an impossibility for them.

So far as British exports were concerned, governmental
encouragement, combined with the very favourable ' sellers'
market ' that existed for some years after the war, enabled the
initial target of 175 per cent of pre-war to be achieved as early
as 1950.   The devaluation of the pound in 1949 also helped
this by cheapening exports, but the effect of such a measure
could not be permanent.   Progress consequently slowed down
after 1950, and the volume of exports which in 1950 was 177
per cent of 1946 (and approximately the same percentage of
the pre-war figure) was only about steady in the early 1950's.
German and Japanese competition began to be felt, particularly in the sphere of motor exports and textiles ; and the
most successful export industries, in terms of growth, were
aircraft, chemicals, motor cars, engineering and electrical
goods, and iron and steel.   Each of these was a more substantial earner of foreign currency than the old staples, cotton
and wool, both of which actually declined and for a time at
least (early in 1952) suffered from serious unemployment.
Owing to the increasing number of transatlantic visitors, the
British tourist industry made a notable contribution to the
closing of the so-called ' dollar gap ' ; and the American
dollar contributions to the British rearmament programme and
to the maintenance costs of American air forces in Britain,
where they had again been stationed since 1949, had a similar
effect.

For if Britain was economically dependent on the United
States, she was also thrown into closer and closer association
with her transatlantic partner in the sphere of foreign policy.

Plate 15 THE LATER 1940's.
(*Left*) The wedding of
Princess Elizabeth and
Lt. Philip Mountbatten,
1947.   (*Below*) Clement
Attlee (left) and Ernest
Bevin, 1950.

Plate 16 SCIENTIFIC ADVANCE. (*Above*) Frank Whittle explaining the mechanism of a jet engine, 1948. (*Below*) The atomic power station at Calder Hall, 1956.

To a large extent it was the attitude of the Soviet Government under Stalin which had brought about this state of affairs. At first it had been hoped that the three major powers, Britain, America, and Russia, would be able to co-operate together in shaping the post-war world. The satisfactory functioning of the United Nations Organisation, which they had brought into existence in 1945, depended upon this, as did the prospect of securing peace treaties and an early reconstruction for the defeated powers. Unfortunately Russian suspicion and intransigence prevented agreement either in the United Nations or by direct negotiation between the major powers. There were three major turning-points of post-war foreign policy for Britain. The first was the offer of Marshall Aid, and the Russian refusal to co-operate in the plans for its distribution in Europe. The second was the Communist *coup d'état* in Czechoslovakia in February 1948—an event which reminded British people most unpleasantly of events nine years earlier. The third was the attempt by the Russian occupation forces in Germany in the summer of 1948 to deny the Western powers any access to their sectors of Berlin—an act that was overcome only by an improvised ' air lift ' of supplies.

In the face of any threat from Russia, western Europe looked like a power vacuum, for American and British occupation forces in Germany had been drastically cut, and the other countries were weak and disunited. Britain and France signed a treaty of alliance in 1947, and in the following year by the Brussels Agreement Belgium, the Netherlands, and Luxembourg were brought in. But in 1949 this was enormously strengthened by the establishment of a North Atlantic Treaty Organisation (NATO), which comprised all the powers of the European Atlantic seaboard with the exception of Eire [1] and Spain, in association with the United States and Canada and three Mediterranean powers—Italy, Greece, and Turkey. This was the first military alliance made by the United States since 1778, and the most comprehensive to which Britain had ever committed herself. A Supreme Headquarters of Allied Powers in Europe (SHAPE) was constituted at Paris, and all the participating powers undertook to contribute forces to

[1] The former Irish Free State, which in 1949 declared itself a completely independent republic.

serve under this command. British forces were to remain in Germany, although West Germany in 1954-5 became a full member of the organisation and contributed forces of her own. American troops were also to stay in Europe, substantially reinforced.

It was hoped that these measures would keep the Russians at bay. The struggle to secure this object became known as ' the cold war ', and the policy was spoken of as a policy of ' containment '. At first the best guarantee of security for the Western nations appeared to be the American monopoly of the atomic bomb, but the Russians came to share this secret in 1949. After this the main deterrent seemed to be the possession by the West of so wide a variety of bases that they could never be eliminated at once by a surprise attack. The security of any particular country—and especially of a geographically small country such as Britain—seemed to be more and more difficult to ensure if atomic war should break out. This became even more obvious when the hydrogen bomb was invented and tested in 1952 and 1953 by the United States and Russia almost simultaneously. As for Britain, she did her best to keep up with the two major powers, using testing grounds in Australia or in the Pacific ; and she exploded an atomic bomb in 1952, and in 1955 embarked on the production of the hydrogen bomb. She thus in a certain sense retained her status as a great power. But the Government was driven to acknowledge that adequate air defence for the population was impossible, so that all depended on the deterrent, and if it failed to deter there seemed to be no alternative to mutual destruction.

Strategical considerations of this character, as well as the economic difficulties of the country, gave added weight to a movement for the political unification of Europe—or at least Europe outside the zone of Russian control. In the later 1940's Winston Churchill, then out of office, helped to inspire the movement, and as a result of some negotiation between governments a first step was taken by the establishment in 1949 of a ' Council of Europe ' at Strasbourg. Its membership of ten included some of the central European nations which were not members of NATO ; and it comprised a Council of Ministers and also a Consultative Assembly drawn from the parliaments of the several countries. But the Council of Europe won no executive powers from the European governments, for few of them and least of all Britain were as yet prepared for the merging of sovereignties which the conception of 'united Europe' implied.

Britain, of course, was still a power with world-wide interests and commitments, although the strain of maintaining them permanently as they were in 1945 could not be contemplated. It was perhaps fortunate that the Government which came into office in that year was anxious to help the more developed parts of the dependent Empire to acquire their independence ; for this was inevitably the trend of the times. It would have been impossible for Britain to have held down by force the burgeoning nationalist movements of her Asiatic possessions ; and it was the recognition of this fact that enabled her ministers to deal rapidly with the final phases of transition to independence in India, Ceylon, and Burma. What was very remarkable, however, was that three of the four states that came into existence as a result—India, Pakistan, and Ceylon, though not Burma—elected to remain as members of the British Commonwealth of Nations.

The most difficult issue in these changes was the communal problem in India, and this led to the creation of the separate state of Pakistan which was carved out of the predominantly Muslim areas. Negotiations on this problem had seemed in danger of collapse when Attlee in February 1947—at the height of Britain's winter fuel crisis—declared that whatever happened there would be a transfer of power from British hands in June 1948. This brought the various Indian leaders —Gandhi, Nehru, and Jinnah in particular—to a recognition of their immediate responsibilities ; and Lord Mountbatten, who was appointed the last Viceroy of India, effectively combined his great prestige as a member of the Royal Family and his qualities of imagination and energetic action in order to surmount the final administrative problems. The transfer of power over a population of some four hundred million— one-sixth of the world's total population—thus took place smoothly ; and though it was followed by some months of cruel strife between the Hindu and Muslim communities, which led to many deaths and much hardship, it nevertheless

brought into existence two important new states, one of them
—India herself—now playing a major role in world diplomacy.
Ceylon and Burma had already achieved their independence
in the course of 1947. But British control continued in Malaya
and Singapore, where a plural society made the development
of a genuine nationalism difficult. In Malaya guerilla warfare
against the Government was begun in 1948 by Malayan-
Chinese Communists, whose bases in the jungle proved almost
impossible to detect or destroy. But owing to the dollar-
earning capacity of Malayan exports (rubber and tin) Britain
had strong reasons for not wanting to give up the struggle.

Naturally the threat of Communist expansion which
menaced the countries of western Europe was strongly felt in
Asia. The victory of the Chinese Communists in their civil
war against Chiang Kai Shek took place in 1949, and at once
transformed the political situation in neighbouring countries.
In the summer of 1950 the Communist leaders of North Korea,
which had been occupied by Russian forces, invaded South
Korea, from which American troops had just been withdrawn.
This aggression was condemned by the United Nations
Organisation, in the absence of Russian representatives who
had unwisely decided to boycott its meetings. Thus the
United States was able to intervene as the agent of the United
Nations to save the South Koreans ; and Britain and other
countries which were her allies supported her with small
contingents. The war which followed developed into a long
and chequered struggle against not only North Koreans but
also Chinese 'volunteers', strengthened by Russian arms.
The line was stabilised in 1951 close to the original boundary
between North and South Korea, but an armistice was not
finally achieved until July 1953. In this unpleasant and
inconclusive war the Americans lost 25,000 killed ; and
Britain lost 600. Afterwards in 1954, on the initiative of the
United States, a South-East Asia Treaty Organisation (SEATO)
was formed as a counterpart to NATO, and Britain as well as
Pakistan, Australia, and New Zealand—but not India or
Burma—took part in this.

The Middle East remained a sphere of considerable British
interest, owing to its oil resources on which Britain was
increasingly dependent, and because of the importance of the

Suez Canal to British shipping. But Arab nationalism challenged British influence, and the special problem of Jewish immigration into Palestine—which was still under British mandate in 1945—prevented any peaceful settlement in the area. At first the British Government tried to associate the United States with its policy for Palestine, but it failed, and in the end as the Jewish and Arab populations of Palestine became uncontrollable the decision was taken to withdraw all British forces by May 1948. The result was war between Jews and Arabs which ended in the establishment of an independent Jewish state, Israel.

From these events Britain lost prestige throughout the Middle East, and nationalist movements were correspondingly encouraged. The Persians, for instance, denounced their treaty with the Anglo-Iranian Oil Company, which was partly owned by the British Government, and it was not until three years later that they were prepared to come to terms for the continued exploitation of their resources. In Egypt, after a revolution which brought a group of young army officers to the fore, Britain was under heavy pressure to evacuate the Canal Zone, where a large military base had been retained. This was reluctantly agreed to in 1954, to the concern of many Conservative backbenchers known as the ' Suez Group '. It was also agreed that the Anglo-Egyptian condominium of the Sudan should come to an end, and that the Sudanese should have the option of union with Egypt or independence. It was thus only at Aden and a few places in the Persian Gulf that Britain retained control, though Iraq and Turkey remained as her allies.

In Central Africa, where many British responsibilities still existed, the Colonial Office made determined efforts to secure both economic and political development. In this task Creech Jones, the Labour Colonial Secretary, could put into practice some of the ideas which he had helped to shape as Secretary of the Fabian Society's Colonial Bureau before and during the war. Riots in the Gold Coast in 1947 hastened that territory's advance, but its uninterrupted progress towards independence would not have been possible without a vigorously expanding economy and a comparative absence of serious internal disunity. Kwame Nkrumah, the leader of the Convention

People's Party, was able to assume office as Prime Minister in 1951 and retain support throughout the transition period which ended in full independence within the Commonwealth —under a new name, Ghana—in 1957.

Other African territories could not advance as quickly as the Gold Coast. Nigeria, though much larger, was poorer and its population was more heterogeneous ; consequently it remained in a more fully dependent condition. In East Africa generally the issue was complicated by the presence of substantial white minorities. In Kenya native resentment over the land question led to an unpleasant form of terrorism, the Mau Mau, which called for emergency measures in 1952. Farther south, arrangements were made to federate Northern Rhodesia and Nyasaland with Southern Rhodesia—a change strongly opposed by African opinion but favoured by the Colonial Office for the sake of the economic development of the territories concerned. Suspicions were increased by the policy of the South African Government, which introduced *apartheid* or racial segregation ; and the British Government was embarrassed by this in its administration of the adjoining territories—particularly Bechuanaland, where it felt obliged to depose and exile Chief Seretse Khama, who had married a white woman.

The tendency towards autonomy in the dependent Empire, however, was plain enough ; and the Commonwealth of Nations steadily gained members at the expense of the Colonial Office's responsibilities. Apart from Eire only Burma was entirely lost to the association in this period ; but India became a republic, and Pakistan seemed to intend to become a caliphate. King George VI ceased to be Emperor of India, and his successor, Queen Elizabeth II, who came to the throne in 1952, was greeted as ' Head of the Commonwealth '. In some ways the unity of the Commonwealth was weakened by the greater diversity of the countries inside it, and by their tendency to develop their own independent policies. But the Commonwealth Conferences continued to be held at periodic intervals and to secure an almost complete attendance of Prime Ministers. The coronation of the Queen in June 1953 provided striking evidence of their willingness to bear witness to the continuing tradition.

Many of the contributions that Britain had already made

to the building of the Commonwealth nations were reinforced at this period. Emigration to the areas of white settlement went on at a rate of about 100,000 a year. This was to some extent offset by immigration, which however differed in being partly a movement of Asiatics or Negroes—a feature that developed particularly in the 1950's. Britain provided for the Commonwealth countries much help in the training of technicians, in university education, and in the equipment of their armed forces. Though private investment abroad was at a low level, the successive British Governments sought to make some provision for public investment in the Commonwealth. The need to find non-dollar sources of food combined with altruistic motives to inaugurate two important schemes under the Overseas Food Corporation—one for raising groundnuts in East Africa and one for growing fodder in Queensland, Australia. Unfortunately the groundnuts scheme ran into unexpected difficulties and had to be abandoned. Various less ambitious schemes for local improvement were also carried out, from funds made available by the British Government through the Colonial Development Corporation, and also through the wider Colombo Plan, to which the Canadian and Australian Governments made contributions.

The responsibility for helping the poorer Commonwealth countries, and especially the dependent territories, was thus clearly recognised. What was actually done was probably not more than a fair return for the contribution made by the colonies to the international position of sterling. But much remained to be done ; and it was becoming increasingly clear that the economic welfare of the backward parts of the Commonwealth, like its entire financial structure and military defence, required the close and generous co-operation of the United States if it were to make any noteworthy progress.

★

Attlee's Labour Cabinet, as at first constituted in 1945, had twenty members, and thus signalised an abandonment of the small 'War Cabinet' system. But he did not entirely discard the policy of limiting the size of the major decision-making bodies : he gave special powers to a number of senior ministers, some of them without departmental responsibilities, to undertake the co-ordination of policy in particular spheres. Thus Herbert Morrison as Lord President of the Council was to supervise the programme of nationalisation ; Arthur Greenwood as Lord Privy Seal was to be primarily responsible for the extension of the social services ; and Ernest Bevin as Foreign Secretary assumed a wide suzerainty over all external affairs. Dalton as Chancellor of the Exchequer rather uneasily shared the field of economic policy with Sir Stafford Cripps, who was President of the Board of Trade. Attlee himself held the Ministry of Defence until after demobilisation, when he passed it to A. V. Alexander.

The Government at once proceeded to its promised legislative programme. In this, nationalisation took up much of the time : the Bank of England was taken over in 1946, and at the end of the same year the coal industry was placed in the hands of the National Coal Board, a semi-autonomous authority under the Minister of Fuel and Power. Another Act established two public corporations for civil aviation. In 1947 a British Transport Commission was established to assume control of the railways, canals, and road haulage of the country. Under the Commission a Road Haulage Executive was set up to run a new service, British Road Services, which took over all goods traffic by road except that undertaken by firms carrying their own merchandise. In 1948 the British Electricity Authority, with Area Electricity Boards, came into existence to run the electricity industry, and in the following year the British Gas Council and Area Gas Boards were constituted.

These measures effectively completed the promised nationalisation programme except for iron and steel. This industry presented some difficulties, not only because it was a comparatively efficient industry in its existing condition, but also because many of the firms concerned in it had major interests in other industries. In order to provide time for the consideration of this issue at a later stage in the Parliament's life, without losing the chance of enacting legislation, the Government first decided to reduce the delaying power of the House of Lords. A bill for this purpose, cutting the Lords' right of postponement of legislation from three successive sessions (as under the 1911 Act) to two, was passed into law in 1949. The Government's Iron and Steel Act, which provided for the retention of the existing structure of the industry under national ownership, was also passed in the 1949 session amid bitter Conservative opposition ; the Lords, though unable to stop its enactment, secured a postponement of the vesting date to February 1951.

Nationalisation clearly had certain advantages for the co-ordination of services in the industries concerned, and for the planning of capital investment in them. Yet the publicly owned industries were expected to prove individually profitable, and there was some wasteful competition between them—for instance, between the gas and electricity industries—which was not eliminated. But the major disappointments of nationalisation were for the workers in the industries concerned. Although conditions often markedly improved, the executives and managements largely consisted of the same people as under private enterprise, and the ideal of ' workers' control ' seemed as far off as ever. Nor could nationalisation in itself do anything to achieve the equalisation of incomes, as some Socialists had vaguely hoped : for the experts who were necessary to run them had to be paid salaries which were to some extent competitive with those obtainable in private industry—and private industry still amounted to 80 per cent of the total industry of the country. Furthermore, the former owners of the nationalised industries had to be paid a reasonable compensation for the loss of their property. It thus became apparent that in spite of the appointment of a few leading trade unionists to the new public boards, nationalisation could as yet do little to transform the character of British society.

Under these circumstances the Government's achievements in the spheres of education, the social services, and finance assumed greater importance. In education the most that could be done was to try to ensure that the 1944 Act, unlike the 1918 Act, was implemented. In 1947 the school-leaving age was at last raised to 15, but little else could be achieved owing to the shortage of staff and buildings. The social services were very much extended, partly by the Minister of National Insurance, James Griffiths, and partly by the Minister of Health, Aneurin Bevan. Griffiths's National Insurance Act of 1946 followed the Beveridge recommendations by consolidating existing legislation and by abolishing the system of approved societies which dated from the Act of 1911. Bevan's Housing Acts of 1946 and 1949 facilitated a policy of publicly assisted house-building, almost to the exclusion of private building. The whole question of housing became highly contentious, owing to the acute shortage, and the Government's failure to achieve an annual total of 200,000 new houses was much criticised.

Even more contentious was Bevan's National Health Service Act of 1946, which was at first strongly opposed by the general practitioners because it seemed to threaten their professional freedom. The Act established a free medical service for all, with doctors and dentists receiving capitation fees for the patients that they undertook to treat. ' Health centres ' or public clinics were envisaged, but there was no immediate prospect of money and resources being available for their construction. The voluntary hospitals were now taken over by the state and organised under regional boards. Drugs, medicine, and appliances were supplied free, and the passing of the Act was followed by an extraordinary public demand for dentures, spectacles, and other aids. The expense of the scheme to the Exchequer was consequently much more than had been anticipated, although the gain in national efficiency that resulted could not be similarly measured. The facilities provided by the scheme often remained inadequate, but they were widely appreciated by the public ; and it was noteworthy that the Conservative Party promised to maintain the service if it were returned to power in 1950.

The policy of the Treasury in this period was again discovered to be one of the most important influences in transforming British society. Hugh Dalton, Attlee's first Chancellor, and Stafford Cripps, who succeeded him in 1947, were not averse to using it for this purpose. They retained the system of direct taxation which had existed during the war, with its steeply rising rates for higher incomes, and this provided a much larger proportion of their budgets than it had done for pre-war Chancellors. Much of it was returned to the taxpayers collectively in the form of increased social services or food subsidies, which were redistributive in effect. Working-class earnings also benefited considerably, by comparison with pre-war, through the maintenance of full employment : the total of unemployed was hardly ever above 400,000. Dalton's ' cheap money ' policy, designed to encourage local government borrowing for housing and other projects, had grave disadvantages : it resulted in a rapid rise in the capital values of industrial shares, and so gave a substantial untaxed bonus to the wealthier sections of the community, besides increasing inflationary pressure. It was already being abandoned when in 1947 Dalton made an indiscreet disclosure about a proposed budgetary change and so had to resign. The policies of his successor, Sir Stafford Cripps, provided the ' austerity ' for all classes of the community which was necessary to deal with the dollar gap.

The other work of the Labour Government was less important, if not always less controversial. In 1946 it repealed the Trades Disputes Act of 1927, and restored the trade unions' right, as established by the Act of 1913, to affiliate their membership to the Labour Party on a ' contracting-out ' basis. This meant an immediate large increase in the funds of the Labour Party ; but its main purpose was psychological—to enable the labour movement to ' get its own back ' for what it had always regarded as an unjust reprisal after the General Strike. A New Towns Act of 1946 empowered the Government to undertake the development of several entirely new towns, most of them to house Londoners in new communities outside the immediate area of Greater London. An Atomic Energy Act of the same year gave the Minister of Supply authority to develop the resources of the atom for peaceful uses. A Representation of the People Act of 1948 abolished the university and business votes, improved the arrangements for registration, and redistributed the seats to take account of population changes. Another Act of the same year established a Monopolies Commission to inquire into cases where monopolistic practices ran counter to the public interest.

The Government's hesitations in the sphere of defence policy were much criticised. In 1947 it introduced legislation for peace-time conscription for an eighteen-month period, but was faced by a revolt of its own backbenchers, many of whom

felt that the period was too long. It therefore changed the
period to twelve months. In 1948, however, increased international tension led to a decision to revert to eighteen months ;
and in 1950, after the outbreak of the Korean War, it became
two years. The period might have been reduced if recruitment
for regular service had not been very sluggish.

Public opinion probably judged the Government primarily
by its success or failure in improving the general standard of
living. In these few years nationalisation could make no
difference one way or the other ; but the expansion of the
social services, together with the maintenance of full employment, did enable an important advance to take place. On
the other hand the continued food shortages and rationing of
goods and materials were exasperating : and in 1950 prices
were beginning to rise steeply. Attlee himself, though a good
chairman of the Cabinet, entirely lacked the oratorical abilties
of Churchill.

The expected general election took place in February 1950.
There was a very large number of candidates, for the Conservative and Labour Parties fought almost every seat, the
Liberals more than three-quarters of them, and the Communists a full hundred. But sample polls—largely a post-war
novelty—showed that Conservatives and Labour were neck
and neck, and so their other rivals fared badly. Over two-
thirds of the Liberals and all but three of the Communists lost
their deposits.[1] Compared with 1945 there was a 3 per cent
turnover of votes from Labour to the Conservatives, but this
was not enough to deprive Labour of an overall majority. In
the new House the Labour Party held 315 seats ; the Conservatives and their allies 297 ; and there were 9 Liberals.
The striking feature of the result was the balance between the
two major parties, and the almost complete elimination of
Liberals and Independents.

Under the circumstances Attlee had to continue in office,
but it was clear that he could not initiate any very contentious
legislation. The projects for further nationalisation which had
been contemplated—sugar, cement, water supplies among them
—had to be put aside ; as it was, the Labour whips found it

[1] £150 each. This penalty was imposed by the 1918 Act on all
candidates who failed to secure one-eighth of the votes cast.

difficult to avoid defeat in key divisions such as those on the clauses of the budget. There were often long and violent debates, particularly as the Government allowed the Iron and Steel Act to go into operation; and the strain on Ministers and Members alike was severe. On several occasions over 600 M.P.s voted, out of a total House membership of 625.

In July 1950 the party strife was overshadowed by the outbreak of the Korean War. This led to new measures of rearmament, which were supported by the Opposition. It was of importance for the Government's future, however, that the rise in the cost of raw materials and in the level of shipping charges accelerated the rise in domestic prices. The rearmament programme also led indirectly to a split in the Government, for Hugh Gaitskell, who had succeeded the ailing Cripps at the Exchequer, found it necessary to make economies in the National Health Service by placing a 50 per cent charge on the supply of spectacles and dentures, and this caused Aneurin Bevan and Harold Wilson to resign. This was especially unfortunate at a time when Attlee's Cabinet had just lost its two strongest figures, Bevin and Cripps, owing to illness, and when the Prime Minister himself was in bad health. All these difficulties, and an impending Commonwealth tour by the King (whose presence was desirable at any political turning-point) led Attlee to ask for a dissolution in September 1951.

The 1951 election campaign was comparatively uneventful. There were considerably fewer Liberal, Communist, or Independent candidates; and the only real acrimony was that provoked by the accusation occasionally made against the Conservatives that they were 'war-mongers'. On election day the *Daily Mirror* hinted at this in an article entitled 'Whose finger on the trigger?' Probably, however, domestic issues bulked more with the electors: the continued shortages, including that of houses, and the rising prices. Compared with 1950 a further swing of 1 per cent of the total vote took place. Although the Labour Party still had the highest total vote of all parties, too high a proportion of its supporters were concentrated in 'safe' seats instead of in the hotly contested 'marginal' areas. The Conservatives and their allies thus became the largest party in the House with a total of 321;

Labour held 295 ; and the Liberals fell to 6. The trends shown in the previous election had all been continued ; and it was now the Conservative responsibility to take office with a small majority.

Winston Churchill, now aged 77, became Prime Minister once more after a gap of six and a half years. He formed a Cabinet of sixteen members—only one smaller than Attlee's last ; but he reverted to his old wartime methods in assuming personally the Ministry of Defence, and in appointing a number of senior co-ordinating ministers—Lord Woolton for Food and Agriculture, Lord Leathers for Transport, Fuel and Power, and Lord Cherwell for Atomic Production and Research and for Statistics. All these ' overlords ' as they were dubbed were members of the House of Lords—a fact somewhat resented by the Opposition. But a number of younger Commons men with a distinctly modern outlook were placed in key administrative posts—R. A. Butler at the Exchequer, Sir Walter Monckton as Minister of Labour, and Harold Macmillan as Minister of Housing were the obvious examples.

The new ministry's policies at first seemed to differ little from those of its predecessor. This was partly because it had to face the same external difficulties, starting off with a fresh balance-of-payments crisis at the end of 1951. Butler's policy could not differ very markedly from that of Gaitskell, who had been the last Labour Chancellor : and people soon learned to speak of ' Butskellism ' as the sort of Treasury attitude which could survive a change of government. There was not much difference in principle between Gaitskell's charges for National Health appliances and Butler's cuts in the food subsidies, which came in the budget of 1952. Then again, the comparatively small size of the Government's parliamentary majority obliged it to keep its more contentious legislation to the minimum. It did not take very long to abandon the idea of reintroducing the university seats to which the Conservatives had pledged themselves at the election. It decided to restore the iron and steel industry to private ownership, and power to do this was provided by legislation in 1953 ; but it appointed an Iron and Steel Board to supervise the industry, so as to ensure that capital development was undertaken when necessary, and it allowed for trade-union representation on the Board. Legislation was also passed to change the Transport Act so as to allow more scope for private road-haulage operators ; but the new publicly owned British Road Services were not by any means entirely dismembered.

This moderate policy, combined with dissensions in the Opposition, made the Government popular with public opinion, at any rate from 1952 onwards. The Labour Party seemed to be divided into warring factions : on the one hand were the ' Bevanites ' whose colourful leader, Aneurin Bevan, advocated policies that appealed to the rank-and-file constituency workers ; on the other hand was an aging leadership, under Attlee and Morrison, supported by the big voting battalions of the larger trade unions. By contrast the Conservatives displayed, at least on the surface, a steady loyalty to their leader, whose position was virtually unchallengeable so long as he cared to retain it, and whose vitality and vigour belied all gloomy prognostications. It was also the Government's good fortune that after 1951 there was a very considerable improvement in the external balance of payments, due to a fall in the cost of raw materials, which greatly benefited the British side of the ' terms of trade '. Consequently the rising price of foodstuffs, which followed Butler's cuts in the food subsidies, did not get out of hand ; and in 1955 he was able to undertake some tax reductions, bringing the income tax down by 6d to 8s 6d. Meanwhile Harold Macmillan as Minister of Housing had the satisfaction of achieving the Government's promised target of 300,000 houses a year.

There were, it is true, a considerable number of industrial disputes, as a result of the rising cost of living. In 1953 the Confederation of Shipbuilding and Engineering Unions undertook a one-day token strike ; in 1954 there was a good deal of trouble at the docks ; and in 1955 serious disputes took place in London newspaper printing, which shut down most of the morning papers, and on the railways, where the engine-drivers threatened and eventually undertook a national strike. But the Government did not on balance suffer in public esteem as a result, for much of the trouble was due to disagreements over jurisdiction or over wage differentials between different unions.

Meanwhile the public had concentrated much of its

attention in 1953 on the coronation of Queen Elizabeth II, and at the end of the year the young Queen with her husband, the Duke of Edinburgh, proceeded on a world tour. The death of Stalin in the same year had opened up the possibility of fresh contacts between the heads of government of the Great Powers, and Winston Churchill, though aging, remained in office in the hope of participating in these. His Government was sufficiently well favoured by the public to increase its vote at some of the by-elections, and even to win a seat from the Opposition. Consequently he had no wish to retire until the actual onset of physical infirmity. He celebrated his eightieth birthday while still Prime Minister in November 1954, and only finally stepped down in April 1955. His successor was Anthony Eden, who appointed Harold Macmillan as his own successor at the Foreign Office, and decided in favour of an immediate general election.

Polling took place in May 1955, in an atmosphere of political apathy and, on the whole, contentment. Both major parties lost votes, and the total poll declined from 82·6 per cent in 1951 to 76·8. But the Labour Party lost a larger proportion of its supporters than the Conservatives did, and this had the effect of a ' swing ' to the Conservatives—the first occasion in peacetime, since the financial influence of the Crown on politics disappeared, that a government which had already served a term had been able to improve its position at a general election. The Conservatives and their allies increased the number of their seats from 319 at dissolution to 345 ; Labour declined from 293 to 277 ; and the Liberals remained constant at 6. A stable Conservative Government was thus guaranteed for a further term.

*

After the exciting times of war the aftermath of peace often seems disappointing ; and for many people Britain after 1945 was no exception to this. The country had still a formidable struggle on its hands—the struggle for economic solvency ; but economic statistics could not prove as inspiring as the tide of war. Demobilisation of the forces was carefully planned, on a basis of age and service except for certain key tradesmen ; and each ex-serviceman received a gratuity and a set of utility clothing on his return to civilian life. But he found that in ' Civvy Street ' there was an acute housing shortage, and that the rations, which were much less substantial than service rations, were in some ways becoming even more meagre. Bread rationing was introduced in March 1946 and potato rationing in November 1947.

It was in the winter of 1946-7 that the country experienced the worst of its shortages. This was an exceptionally severe winter, with a great deal of snow ; and in February the coal stocks which were already low could not be replenished because of transport difficulties due to the bad weather. For several days much of the industry of the country had to close down ; almost two million people were temporarily unemployed ; and domestic use of electricity was forbidden during normal working hours. The foreign exchange crisis later in 1947 led to a complete ban on the use of foreign currency for tourist travel ; and the basic petrol ration for private motoring was suspended.

Gradually after 1947 the situation eased, although there were ups and downs due to the almost biennial balance-of-payments crisis. Bread, potatoes, and jam were taken off the ration in 1948 ; clothes and footwear in 1949 ; milk and soap in 1950. But sugar and tea remained until late 1952 ; and butter, fats, bacon, and meat until 1954. Many other controls remained long after the Labour Government had fallen, and some—particularly those involving the purchase of goods from dollar countries—seemed likely to be long-lived. Home agriculture remained heavily subsidised, and did substantially improve its output of meat, dairy produce, and wheat.

In this situation of scarcity and ' austerity ', successive governments paid much attention to the problems of industrial productivity. Under the Marshall Plan teams of British executives and trade unionists visited America to study methods of achieving greater efficiency. To encourage greater understanding of the problems involved, the annual *Economic Survey* was published by the Government, with a popular edition as well. A permanent British Productivity Council was set up, and a good deal more attention was paid to training for management and to the ' human relations ' aspect of factory employment. Joint consultation between management and workers became much more widespread, and was largely responsible for the general reduction in the number of industrial disputes that caused strikes or lock-outs. Many of the disputes which did lead to strikes were caused, as we have seen, either by disputes between unions over jurisdiction—and here the Transport and General Workers, the largest of the unions, was often involved—or over wage differentials, for unskilled workers had improved their incomes very considerably in relation to the skilled. There were many observers who demanded a rationalisation of the union pattern, or a ' national wages policy ' ; but neither of these proposals was very practicable while the individual unions retained so much power. Consequently nothing was done, though the Government often called upon the movement to exercise ' restraint ' in pressing wage claims—not without success, at least in the first years after the war.

One reason why voluntary ' wage restraint ' could be hoped for and to some extent achieved was that wage rates had gone up rapidly during the war ; and with the addition of the increased social service benefits the working population was enormously better off than before the war. Seebohm Rowntree found that whereas in 1936 31 per cent of the working population of York was below a ' poverty-line ' of his own calculation, in 1950 only 2·77 per cent were below it. These remaining unfortunates were mostly old-age pensioners, who had not benefited as much as wage-earners in general. Full employment had a good deal to do with the improvement. The introduction of the National Health Service, combined with the rapid advance in medical technique, also made a great difference to social welfare. The infantile mortality rate dropped from 55 per thousand in 1938 to 26 in 1954—which put Britain, temporarily at least, ahead of the United States, though still behind Holland or Sweden. The new drugs had virtually eliminated infectious disease as a cause of death, except for poliomyelitis ; and the tuberculosis rate was dropping to almost negligible proportions, largely as a result of preventive ' mass radiography '.

Generally speaking, however, the popularity of Socialist planning, even as advocated by the more moderate members of the Labour Party, declined considerably in these years—as might be inferred from the election results. Planning became associated with the continuing shortages, with which most people, and especially the housewife, became heartily ' fed up '. For one thing, shortages encouraged the existence of a ' black market ', which for some people prepared to risk illegality (the ' spivs ' as they were called) brought quick profits in return for little effort. Nationalisation, as we have seen, proved disillusioning ; and even several years after the establishment of the National Coal Board, coal was being imported from foreign countries—sometimes even from the United States. The intransigence of Russian foreign policy in the last years of Stalin also increased the unpopularity of the Left in general. Literature tended sharply to the right : Catholic authors such as Graham Greene and Evelyn Waugh were popular ; and the biting satire of George Orwell, directed primarily against Left-totalitarianism in his post-war works *Animal Farm* (1945) and *1984* (1949), made a strong impression.

It would not be true, however, to say that there was very much enthusiasm for Conservatism as such. The Conservative Party received increased support in the later forties from people angered by the restrictions of the time or by the incautious remarks of Labour ministers, but for the most part there was a general decline in political enthusiasm, which became particularly marked at the end of the period. It was felt that after the reforms of the first post-war Government things at home were not really worth getting angry about— especially as many of the difficulties were caused by the external situation ; and it seemed that Britain was no longer free to conduct her own foreign policy, for what happened in the world depended largely on Russia and the United States. The threat of ' the bomb '—first the atomic bomb, then the even more alarming hydrogen bomb—aroused a certain amount of political agitation, particularly on the Left, but its effect on most people was numbing rather than stimulating. Attendance at political meetings dropped, not entirely as a result of the rival attractions of television ; and, as we have seen, the total vote at general elections declined markedly.

The local authorities, to whom the Government had entrusted so many powers, did their best to cope with the most urgent requirements of housing, education, and welfare, but their resources were always thin in relation to demand. The first results of their housing efforts were an ugly crop of prefabricated dwellings, built to last ten years only. The new permanent houses were built according to high standards of specification, but for economy's sake they lacked all distinction of design or quality. The L.C.C. was building great blocks of flats, again mostly undistinguished, but it was also producing some interesting planned neighbourhoods, such as that called after George Lansbury in a bombed area of Stepney. Eventually other towns with large ' blitzed ' areas such as Coventry, Southampton, and Plymouth had something to show in the same way. The L.C.C. was also a pioneer of open-air entertainment in the public parks—even of an open-air sculpture exhibition in Battersea Park. Of its work in promoting the Festival of Britain, more must be said later. Some of its elementary schools looked individual and interesting, though the palm for well-designed schools went by common consent to Hertfordshire County Council.

It was unfortunate, however, that the housing shortage remained acute until the 1950's, for the Government felt obliged to prevent almost all building except factories, schools, and houses to be let by public authorities. There thus developed a shortage of hotels, so that hotel room prices shot up without much improvement of amenities ; this was a serious disadvantage when foreign tourists poured into the country. There were no new cinemas, and queues of film-goers were the longest of all the post-war queues, though in the long run the competition of television made the cinema industry grateful for being unable to build. Wealthier people would perhaps have felt the absence of new private house-building more acutely if they had not been suffering from the ' servant problem ' more than ever before, so that they were often content to live in flats carved out of the stately homes of earlier generations. More and more of the country's hereditary aristocracy discovered that the only way to keep up their old houses was to turn them into museums which the public would pay to visit ; and many estates were handed over entire to the National Trust or the Ministry of Works to look after, while others were bought by public bodies—sometimes boards of nationalised industries—as headquarters or training colleges for staff.

Although there was some diminution in the range of incomes, there were still plenty of people with capital, and, as we have seen, the investor could do well in the early post-war years as a result of Dalton's ' cheap money ' policy. Farmers on the whole benefited considerably from the heavy subsidies of their produce, now a permanent feature of the budget. It was amazing, too, what business ' expense accounts ' could be used for ; and then there were always the rich people from overseas. Consequently the social round reasserted itself, although rather gradually. The Royal Family was reluctant to encourage too much ostentation, and for some years there were no presentations for débutantes at Court. Dinner-dances were crippled so long as meals were restricted in price to 5s and clothes were rationed. But racing soon revived, and the universities, now more than ever crowded with undergraduates, resumed their sporting events and their annual balls.

Foreign travel, as we have seen, was very restricted at first ; but it became popular with wider and wider sections of the population, although those who were short of foreign languages tended to stick to the organised tours. At first many people who could not go abroad had to make do with French and Italian films, which happened to be of high quality at the end of the war, and consequently experienced a vogue. Later on air travel took people quickly on their Continental holidays, and the improved Continental roads also gave British motor tourists a wider range. Italy, Spain, and Yugoslavia were visited by many. They brought back with them a keener taste for wine, for out-of-door cafés if the weather permitted, and for late-night coffee drinking. The ' espresso ' coffee-shops that mushroomed in the middle fifties were a response to this.

Post-war British films, stimulated by wartime subsidies, were of higher quality than before : Carol Reed's versions of Graham Greene plots ; David Lean's productions of Dickens ; Laurence Olivier's *Hamlet* ; and the Ealing Studios' comedies starring Alec Guinness—all these made their mark, and proved to be good dollar-earners. J. Arthur Rank emerged as the principal financier of the industry, capable, it seemed, of putting it on a sounder permanent basis. American films continued to predominate in the cinemas, but most of them were lavish rather than good, except for the Disney documentaries. Colour was now increasingly used, and in the fifties the wide-screen technique came in—a necessary innovation to enable the industry to compete with television.

Of the other arts, the theatre flourished even without the long-demanded National Theatre ; London productions seemed almost as numerous as ever, and Shakespeare productions at Stratford prospered largely as a result of the summer tourist trade. American playwrights provided strong competition for the British author, however : slick and colourful musicals crossed the Atlantic, beginning with *Oklahoma* in 1947, and with them came the social realism of works such as those by Tennessee Williams or Arthur Miller. In the fifties the sudden success of *The Boy Friend*, a light-hearted British play about the 1920's by Sandy Wilson, was significant : it seemed to imply the passing of the serious post-war years.

The other arts needed lavish patronage, and in the new circumstances this had to come from public bodies. The B.B.C. played a major part in this, especially after the introduction of its Third Programme in 1946, which was designed to cater for a limited highbrow audience—and to widen it if possible. The B.B.C. also continued its work in the encouragement of classical music, including the sponsoring of the Henry Wood Promenade Concerts. The British Council was given the task of ' exporting ' British culture abroad at the taxpayers' expense, and contemporary art and artists benefited from this. The Arts Council, which replaced the wartime CEMA, sponsored or helped to sponsor many activities at home, including the productions of the Sadlers Wells and Covent Garden opera (Benjamin Britten's *Peter Grimes* was produced in the first post-war year) ; the Sadlers Wells Ballet, in which Margot Fonteyn was the supreme performer ; and the work of various orchestras in London and the provinces. It also played a part in helping to start the Edinburgh Festival of Music and Drama, which first took place in 1947 and thereafter became an annual feature, of great value to the tourist industry as well as to the arts. Another part of its work was to help to organise special exhibitions of art from abroad—French tapestries, Van Gogh pictures, Munich and Vienna paintings—which in the early post-war years were some compensation to culture-hungry Britons for their lack of foreign currency. The Institute of Contemporary Art undertook the responsibility of encouraging the work of living artists with *avant-garde* tendencies. Literature, for the most part, was left to the ordinary commercial publishers to sponsor ; on the whole it prospered, and although book prices rose considerably they never approached the American level. Older novelists such as Joyce Carey, L. P. Hartley, and Angus Wilson made their mark, and so did younger ones such as those who commented more specifically on the new post-war world— Kingsley Amis and John Wain among others.

For some years after the end of the war the Press suffered from a strict rationing of newsprint ; but it did not lack the support of the public. The circulation of the serious weeklies grew rapidly during and after the war, as did that of the better Sunday papers—no doubt an indication of the spread of higher education. But their totals remained small by the side of those of the great popular papers—especially the *Daily Express* and the *Daily Mirror* and the giant of the Sunday Press, the *News of the World*, whose weekly collection of spicy court cases regularly attracted over seven million purchasers. Obviously strong monopolistic tendencies were present : but a Royal Commission on the Press set up by the Labour Government found little constructive to recommend in the way of regulating the Press, except for the establishment by the profession itself of a Press Council with powers to examine and report on any breaches of recognised journalistic standards. Such a Press Council duly came into existence in 1953.

The key event dividing the immediate post-war world from the fifties was probably the Festival of Britain of 1951. This occasion, sponsored partly by the Labour Government and partly by the Labour-controlled L.C.C., was designed to show a glimpse of the best that Britain could produce, as a foretaste of the future when shortages were gone. This it did ; and it also gave the architects their first major opportunity since the war to show what they could do, whether in the spectacular permanent concert hall, the Festival Hall as it came to be called, or in the amusing *décor* of the pleasure gardens at Battersea. A National Film Theatre was also constructed on the site of the Festival, at South Bank, and became a permanent legacy of the Festival, which did not like its predecessor of 1851 pay its way financially, though in other respects it fully justified the hopes of its sponsors.

By the middle 1950's it seemed possible to say that the ' post-war era ' was over and that a new era was beginning. This was partly because the immediate grip of the economic controls and restrictions that accompanied the war had now been loosened or entirely broken. But it was also due to the introduction of new techniques and processes in industry and entertainment which changed the pattern of life—and finally, perhaps most of all, to the emergence of a new generation which had only grown up since the end of the war.

What were the main characteristics of mid-century Britain ? It was a country more heavily urbanised and more industrialised than ever before. Four-fifths of the population lived in urban surroundings ; and the various branches of the metal-working industry employed almost four times as many workers as agriculture, forestry, and fishing combined. Agriculture was mechanised as never before ; but the great advances in production between 1948 and 1955 were in chemicals, vehicles, metal engineering, and electrical goods—all of them industries which, as we have seen, did well in export markets.

Inside Britain the post-war demand for new motor vehicles, long pent up owing to export priority, was being satisfied by the early fifties. By 1954 the total number of motor vehicles licensed had increased by 87 per cent since 1938. More and more people were using their own cars or motor cycles to take them on holiday at home or abroad ; the need for some sort of national road-building was urgent, but nothing had so far been done. The railways were badly in need of modernisation, although they were losing traffic to the roads and had had to close many of their smaller branch lines.

Yet as the fifties went on it became noticeable that fewer people left their homes in the evenings. This was because of the advent of television—a B.B.C. monopoly until 1955, but then opened to the competition of ' sponsored ' programmes under the careful supervision of a new public body, the Independent Television Authority. Television began to have its effect on many other older forms of entertainment—it reduced the cinema queues, cut down the consumption of drink in the 'pubs', and even diminished the size of the crowds at football matches. It may also have discouraged reading, and there was much talk of its probable unfavourable effects on the younger generation—as there usually is when any change in social habits takes place.

Certainly it was noticeable that the generation now growing up under the influence of all these changes was inclined to make its own fashions. The feminine 'new look' of the late forties—the long skirt and emphasised bust—gave way to more youthful, even absurd, experiments in fashion : it was the twenties over again, revived however by people who could not remember the twenties. The light-hearted tone of the time was similar in many ways. Politics were now thought uninteresting, because the party battle seemed largely irrelevant to the remaining social problems at home, and there was little that could be done about 'the bomb'. A certain fatalism set in, not uninfluenced by the French philosophy of 'Existentialism'. 'They'—the rulers of the United States and Russia—were in charge of 'our' destiny : the best that 'we' could do was to enjoy life while it lasted. And that meant, for some, Butlin's holiday-camps ; for others, swimming in the Mediterranean, or skiing in Austria ; for some, calypsos and skiffle groups and jive ; for others, the prolonged relaxation of listening to an L.P. disc (first introduced in 1950).

In spite of the more varied pleasures of this new age, and the greater freedom experienced by most people, some of the old barriers remained. It seemed too crude to speak of them as 'class distinctions', and new words were coined—the 'Establishment', or 'U' and 'non-U'. The educational system, though more equalitarian than before, was still sharply divided into state and private ; and the 1944 Act had introduced another sharp division, by separating eleven-year-old children in the state schools into the 'modern school' and the 'grammar school' streams.

The L.C.C. planned a number of 'comprehensive schools' to keep the 'grammar school' and 'modern school' streams in the same set of buildings, thus facilitating movement from one stream to the other and achieving, it was hoped, a general equality of status. But by 1955 this programme had hardly begun to operate ; and many people felt that it might endanger the quality of grammar-school teaching. Suggestions were made for the rapid expansion of the universities, but for the time being Treasury economy imposed a curb on expansion. In the existing state of affairs there was a heavy loss of talent as each school generation went by, for only 15 per cent of boys and girls stayed in the educational system beyond the age of 16, and not more than 4 per cent went on to a university. The proportions, though substantially higher than before the war, were still very small, and compared unfavourably with those for America, Russia, and other countries. It was inevitable that the system had the effect of perpetuating the social distinctions in the population instead of helping to eliminate them. Both Scotland and Wales were to some extent exceptions to this, and had long been so : but the Englishman continued to be ' branded on the tongue ', as a thoughtful Old Etonian, George Orwell, put it. Thus education, though itself being transformed in various ways, still by its divisions acted as a brake upon the speed of social change in mid-century Britain.

9 Britain in the Later Fifties: Retrospect

WHEN Queen Elizabeth II came to the throne in 1952 there was much talk of a ' new Elizabethan Age '. The suggested comparison, which somehow sounds exhilarating, gains added point from a knowledge of the difficulties of sixteenth-century England—of its perilously balanced finances as well as of its rich culture ; of its anxieties in a world of stronger powers, as well as of its triumphs in pioneering beyond the frontiers of the known world. The period when Britain could regard herself as the greatest world power, virtually unchallengeable and secure, was as we now realise no more than an interlude in her history ; and it was in the period that this book has reviewed that she had once more to adapt herself to life on not more than equal terms with much of the rest of mankind.

The two main themes of this story have in fact been two parallel processes of adaptation. One theme was that of Britain's external difficulties, and her gradual recognition of the need to alter her political and economic relations, not only with her ' Empire ' but with all other nations as well. The other main theme concerned the social and political conflicts at home, and the elimination of various forms of inferiority that existed in the nineteenth century—the freeing of the workers from poverty, unemployment, and servility, of women in general from household restraints and social barriers, of the Welsh and the Irish from their sense of subjection to the English. All of these processes have been accomplished gradually, and with rare exceptions—the question of Ireland being the most notable—have taken place peacefully, thus leaving behind them no unpleasant scars on the body politic. The great and violent shocks of the period have come from a quarter always largely beyond the bounds of effective British influence, let alone control : from the conflicts of the great military powers of Continental Europe. And while the wars to which these conflicts gave rise were going on, the other long-term changes in Britain's external and internal situation were not halted—rather they were accelerated by the strains of mobilisation.

All these various developments took place side by side with each other, influencing each other, usually in a positive direction. None of them—and to this the Irish question is no exception—resulted in the change being as complete as its keenest supporters would have wished, and on any particular issue there were always those who could demand a fresh advance towards some ideal solution. But taken together, all these changes transformed the character of British society and Britain's place in the world. Generally speaking, where relations were simple and hierarchical in the nineteenth century, they have now become complex, with a resulting dispersal of authority. Thus the British Empire used to be governed effectively from Whitehall, under the supreme direction of the Cabinet and a few Civil Servants, whose control over a large proportion of the world's total population was tempered only by the difficulty of communications. Now most of the peoples concerned have received their independence, and relations between them and the people of Britain involve negotiations on equal terms. (The difficulties with Egypt, culminating in 1956 in the Suez operation, have only served to underline this conclusion.) Even if Britain remains in many ways the centre of the Commonwealth of Nations, the name itself implies and recognises a diffusion of power hardly contemplated in Queen Victoria's day.

So too in the domestic sphere, the machinery of government, then simple and limited in scope, has expanded to incorporate many new patterns of representation. The ' voluntary bureaucracy ' parallels the bureaucracies of national and local government, and successfully claims the right to influence legislative and administrative action. The employer has become accustomed to the need for consultation with his workers or their representatives for many of the decisions that he must take. If it sometimes seems that the power of the state has been constantly increasing, so that a wartime Prime

Minister may exercise what would seem to his Victorian predecessor to be dictatorial authority, yet we must bear in mind the extent to which this power depends upon the consent of innumerable people, acting as it were as the lubricant of a machine that otherwise could not work.

Have all these changes been for the better ? We cannot say for sure. Happiness does not necessarily spring either from material progress or from emancipation from the restraints of authority. All the same, these things may provide more possibilities of happiness than before. In spite of new problems of various types—heavy taxation, administration delays, and the ever-present threat of an atomic war—there must be some advantage in a state of things in which those both high and low by birth are mixing more freely than ever before, and when the nation's physical health is constantly improving and its opportunities for useful work and enjoyable recreation are always on the increase. And whatever the limitations of the British policy by comparison with others, no country of anything like equal size can claim to have dealt more successfully with the major problems that have divided its citizens at home and challenged them abroad.

Appendix A

June 1885	Marquess of Salisbury	Conservative
February 1886	W. E. Gladstone	Liberal
August 1886	Marquess of Salisbury	Conservative
August 1892	W. E. Gladstone	Liberal
March 1894	Earl of Rosebery	Liberal
June 1895	Marquess of Salisbury	Unionist
July 1902	A. J. Balfour	Unionist
December 1905	Sir Henry Campbell-Bannerman	Liberal
April 1908	H. H. Asquith	Liberal
May 1915	H. H. Asquith	Coalition
December 1916	D. Lloyd George	Coalition
October 1922	A. Bonar Law	Conservative
May 1923	Stanley Baldwin	Conservative
January 1924	J. Ramsay MacDonald	Labour
November 1924	Stanley Baldwin	Conservative
June 1929	J. Ramsay MacDonald	Labour
August 1931	J. Ramsay MacDonald	National
June 1935	Stanley Baldwin	National
May 1937	Neville Chamberlain	National
May 1940	W. S. Churchill	Coalition
May 1945	W. S. Churchill	Conservative
July 1945	C. R. Attlee	Labour
October 1951	W. S. Churchill	Conservative
April 1955	Sir Anthony Eden	Conservative
January 1957	Harold Macmillan	Conservative

Appendix B

POPULATION FIGURES
(United Kingdom, excluding Southern Ireland)

Date	Total Population (in thousands)	Total Births (in thousands) *	Total Deaths (in thousands) *
1881	1,015	33·6	20·8
1891	34,265	30·6	20·7
1901	38,237	28·6	18·4
1911	42,082	24·6	14·9
1921	44,027	23·1	13·5
1931	46,038	16·3	12·9
1941	48,216†	15·0	15·5
1951	50,225	15·9	12·7

* Three-year averages   † Estimated

Appendix C

PERSONS ON REGISTER OF PARLIAMENTARY ELECTORS
(United Kingdom, including, up to 1922, Southern Ireland)

Date	1892	1906	1918	1929	1945	1955
Men (thousands)	6,161	7,267	12,913	13,650	33,240	34,852
Women (thousands)			8,479	15,196		

Appendix D

INDUSTRIAL PRODUCTION

Date	Coal (million tons)	Electricity (million kw-hours)	Crude Steel (million tons)
1913	287		7,664
1929	258	8,666	9,636
1938	227	24,372	10,398
1947	197	42,580	12,725
1955	222	80,148	19,791

Appendix E

MAIN TENDENCIES OF THE NATIONAL ECONOMY (since 1918)

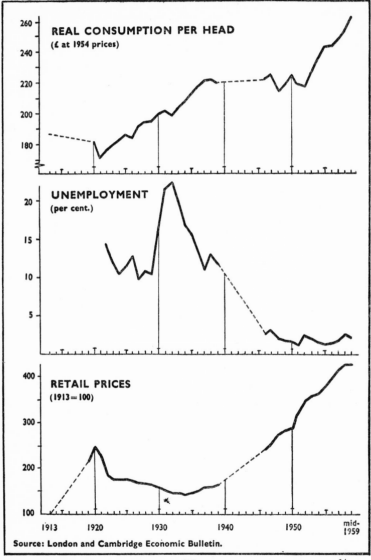

Source: London and Cambridge Economic Bulletin.

Appendix F

EVOLUTION OF THE COMMONWEALTH

In 1885 the areas of the British Empire enjoying ' responsible ' government were : the Australian colonies, New Zealand, Canada, Newfoundland, Cape Colony. Natal secured it in 1893. Thereafter, the major developments in self-government up to 1955 were all embodied in Acts of the United Kingdom Parliament, as follows :

1900   Commonwealth of Australia Constitution Act, establishing federal system.

1909   South Africa Act, forming union of Cape Colony, Natal, Transvaal, and Orange Free State.

1922   Irish Free State Constitution Act.

1931   Statute of Westminster, defining equality of status of certain ' dominions ' with the United Kingdom—namely, Canada, Australia, New Zealand, South Africa, Irish Free State, and Newfoundland.

1947   Ceylon Independence Act.
Indian Independence Act, creating India and Pakistan.
Burma Independence Act. The Union of Burma elected to leave the Commonwealth.

1949   British North America Act, enabling the confederation of Newfoundland with Canada.
Ireland Act, recognising the Republic of Ireland as a state outside the Commonwealth.

In addition, Southern Rhodesia secured internal self-government in 1923, and by the Rhodesia and Nyasaland Federation Act (1953) it was constituted as part of a federation with the Protectorates of Northern Rhodesia and Nyasaland.

Books for Further Reading

General. Good narrative histories covering the whole of this period do not exist ; but two standard volumes cover much of the ground. These are R. C. K. Ensor, *England, 1870–1914* (1936) and C. L. Mowat, *Britain between the Wars, 1918–40* (1955). E. Halévy's *History of the English People : Epilogue* (2 vols., 1934), covering the years 1895–1915, is also valuable.

Economic History. A useful introduction over the long period is W. H. B. Court, *Concise Economic History of Britain from 1750* (1954). J. H. Clapham, *Economic History of Modern Britain*, vol. 3 (1938) is a magisterial survey of the years 1887–1914, with an epilogue running to 1929. See also H. W. Arndt, *Economic Lessons of the Nineteen-Thirties* (1944) and A. Shonfield, *British Economic Policy since the War* (1958). Viscount Astor and B. S. Rowntree, *British Agriculture* (1938) is also helpful. The last two books are in the Penguin Series.

Constitutional History. Probably the best introduction is that afforded by D. L. Keir, *Constitutional History of Modern Britain* (new ed. 1953). Also valuable is E. C. S. Wade's introduction to the ninth edition of A. V. Dicey, *Law of the Constitution* (1939). For the role of the monarch, see F. Hardie, *Political Influence of Queen Victoria* (1938) ; Harold Nicolson, *King George V* (1952) and J. W. Wheeler-Bennett, *King George VI* (1959). W. I. Jennings, *Cabinet Government* (new ed. 1959), D. N. Chester and F. M. G. Willson, *Organisation of British Central Government 1914–56* (1957) and K. B. Smellie, *History of Local Government* (new ed. 1957). Roy Jenkins, *Mr Balfour's Poodle* (1954) is a useful account of the constitutional crisis of 1909–11.

Politics. For changes in the electoral law, see D. E. Butler, *Electoral System in Britain, 1918–51* (1953). The best general urvey of the political parties, although its main thesis is controversial, is R. T. Mackenzie, *British Political Partie* (1955). Histories of the major political parties are as yet lacking, except for G. D. H. Cole's *British Working-Class Politics 1832–1914* (1941) and *History of the Labour Party from 1914* (1948). These may be supplemented by H. Pelling, *Origins of the Labour Party* (1954), F. Bealey and H. Pelling, *Labour and Politics, 1900–06* (1958) and R. W. Lyman, *First Labour Government, 1924* (1957). For the Conservative and Liberal Parties, it is necessary to turn to biographies. This is not the place for a list of these (see Ensor or Mowat), but the older works have been supplemented in recent years by A. L. Kennedy, *Salisbury* (1953), Philip Magnus, *Gladstone* (1954), and R. Rhodes James, *Lord Randolph Churchill* (1959). Lucy Masterman's *C. F. G. Masterman* (1939) has special value for the last Liberal Governments. See also Thomas Jones, *Lloyd George* (1951), Robert Blake, *The*

Unknown Prime Minister: Bonar Law (1955), and Keith Feiling, *Life of Neville Chamberlain* (1946). For the Communist Party, see the *Historical Profile* (1958) by H. Pelling. For the formation of the National Government, see R. Bassett, *1931 : Political Crisis* (1958). On the Labour Government of 1945–51, see E. Watkins, *The Cautious Revolution* (1951).

Social History. On trade unionism, see G. D. H. Cole, *Short History of the British Working-Class Movement* (new ed. 1948) and E. H. Phelps Brown, *Growth of British Industrial Relations* (1959). For social change as illustrated by statistics, see D. C. Marsh, *Changing Social Structure of England and Wales, 1871–1951* (1958), and A. M. Carr-Saunders and others, *Social Conditions in England and Wales* (1958). Inter-war changes are amusingly but informatively described in Robert Graves and Alan Hodge, *The Long Week-end* (1940). For the Suffragettes, see Roger Fulford, *Votes for Women* (1957). Julian Symons, *General Strike* (1957) is also colourful. Asa Briggs, *History of Birmingham*, vol. 2 (1952) unfortunately remains unique as a local study of social change. Other aspects are dealt with in H. C. Barnard, *Short History of English Education* (1947), and G. S. Spinks (ed.), *Religion in Britain since 1900* (1954). For the history of science, see A. E. Heath (ed.), *Scientific Thought in the Twentieth Century* (1952). For literary movements, see W. Y. Tindall, *Forces in Modern British Literature, 1885–1956* (1956). On the press, Francis Williams, *Dangerous Estate* (1957) provides a starting point.

Wales, Scotland, and Ireland. R. Coupland, *Welsh and Scottish Nationalism* (1954) is useful. David Williams, *History of Modern Wales* (1950) and I. M. M. MacPhail, *History of Scotland* (vol. 2, 1956) have introductory value. See also J. A. Bowie, *Future of Scotland* (1939). For Ireland, see N. Mansergh, *Ireland in the Age of Reform and Revolution* (1940), and T. Wilson (ed.), *Ulster under Home Rule* (1955). The Irish Nationalists are ably examined in C. C. O'Brien, *Parnell and his Party* (1957), and F. S. L. Lyons, *Irish Parliamentary Party, 1890–1910* (1951).

Foreign Policy. A useful introduction is provided by M. R. D. Foot, *British Foreign Policy since 1898* (1956). See also P. A. Reynolds, *British Foreign Policy in the Inter-War Years* (1954). On the prelude to the First and Second World Wars respectively, see G. M. Trevelyan, *Grey of Falloden* (1937), and W. S. Churchill, *The Gathering Storm* (1948). For dissenting views of foreign policy, see A. J. P. Taylor, *The Trouble Makers* (1957). For Anglo-German naval rivalry before 1914, see E. L. Woodward, *Great Britain and the German Navy* (1934).

Empire and Commonwealth. An introduction to the subject is provided by C. E. Carrington in his *The British Overseas* (1950). Imperialism at the turn of the century is well analysed in the *Cambridge History of the British Empire*, vol. 3 (1959). Constitutional evolution may be traced in K. C. Wheare, *The Statute of Westminster and Dominion Status* (new ed. 1953) and with more economic background in the extensive but lucid *Survey of British Commonwealth Affairs* by W. K. Hancock and N. Mansergh (4 vols., 1937–58).

War History. Edgar Holt, *The Boer War* (1958) is a vivid and interesting account. Liddell Hart's *War in Outline* (1936) gives a good sketch of Britain's military role in the First World War ; a fuller and more recent work is Cyril Falls, *First World War* (1960). There is no good account of the ' home front ' ; but Lloyd George's *War Memoirs* (6 vols., 1933–6) and Lord Beaverbrook's *Politicians and the War* (2 vols., 1928–32) and *Men and Power* (1956) together with the lives of Bonar Law and King George V already mentioned, give a good picture of war-time politics. For the Second World War, there is a short military history by Cyril Falls, *Second World War* (1948), which may be supplemented by Winston Churchill's own absorbing record, *Second World War* (6 vols., 1948–54). Many aspects of life in war-time Britain are skilfully dealt with in W. K. Hancock and M. M. Gowing, *British War Economy* (1949). J. Ehrman's *Cabinet Government and War* (1958) deals succinctly with the impact of military planning on government in the period 1890–1940.

Significant Biographies and Fiction. The above list omits some of the most significant biographies of the period, which often provide more insights into its problems than books on particular topics. Works such as Beatrice Webb, *My Apprenticeship* (1926), and *Our Partnership* (1948) ; Evelyn Wrench, *Alfred, Lord Milner* (1958) ; R. F. Harrod, *Life of J. M. Keynes* (1951) ; Leslie Paul, *Angry Young Man* (1951) ; and Stephen Spender, *World within World* (1951)—these are all of great interest for different aspects and epochs of modern British history. The same is true of the creative writing of social critics such as George Gissing, H. G. Wells, John Galsworthy, Arnold Bennett, J. B. Priestley, George Orwell, C. P. Snow, and Walter Allen.

Index

Abdication crisis (1936), 127f., 136
Abyssinia, 116, 127, 142f.
Acland, Sir Richard, 153
Adamson, W. M., 95
Aden, 169
Admiral Graf von Spee, 138
Afghanistan, 17, 43
Africa, 14, 17–22, 42, 45, 93, 142f., 169f.,
  and see individual countries
Agadir, 44, 53
Agriculture, 3, 16f., 38, 81, 109, 125,
  181, 188
Aircraft industry, 89, 149, 164
Air Ministry, establishment of, 82f.
Air raids, 79, 83, 152, 156, 157, 161
Air travel, 56, 109
Aitken, Max, see Lord Beaverbrook
Alexander, A. V., 127, 172
Alexander, Gen. H. R. L. G., 144, 146
Algeciras Conference (1906), 43
Allenby, Gen. Sir Edmund, 71
Alsace-Lorraine, 63, 86
America, United States of, see United
  States
Amery, L. S., 149
Amis, Kingsley, 187
'Amritsar massacre' (1919), 93
Anderson, Sir John, 150
Anglo-German naval treaty (1935), 117
Animal Farm (Orwell), 183
Answers, 34
Antwerp, 63, 146, 147
Anzio, 146
'Appeasement', 117
Archangel, 86
Architecture, 36, 60f., 107, 135, 184
'Arcos' raid (1927), 102
Army Bureau of Current Affairs, 161
Army reforms, 43f., 50f., and see Con-
  scription
Arnhem, 147
Arras, 69
Arts Council, 186
Asquith, H. H., Liberal minister, 27,
  49, 50; Prime Minister, 51, 52, 61, 71,

72; fall of, 74f.; in opposition, 76, 78,
  94, 97; leads re-united party, 103
Astor, J. J., 108
Atlantic, Battle of the, 145f.
Atomic bomb, 148, 160, 166, 183, 189
Atomic Energy Act (1946), 175
Attlee, C. R., Labour leader, 127, 149,
  153, 154, 179; Prime Minister, 155,
  167, 171, 174, **176**, 177, 178
Auchinleck, Gen. C. J. E., 143, 144
Auden, W. H., 133
Australia, constitutional status of, 17,
  41; trade with, 3, 14, 17; other refs.,
  5, 20, 39, 144, 166, 168, 171
Austria, 86, 117, 189
Austria-Hungary, 42, 43, 45f.,; in First
  World War, 63, 66, 67, 69, 71
Autobiography (Trollope), 13

Baden-Powell, Col. (*later* Gen.) R. S. S.,
  20, 21, 61
Baghdad railway, 45
Baldwin, Stanley, Conservative Prime
  Minister, 97f., 100, 104; faces party
  revolt, 121; supports National Govern-
  ment, 114, 122, 123; National Prime
  Minister, 116, 117, **126f.**, 128
Balfour, A. J., Conservative leader, 24,
  26, 28; Prime Minister, **47**, 48, 49;
  later career, 53, 72, 95, 97
Bank of England, 112, 172
Barings crisis (1890), 14
Barlow report (1940), 152
Barnes, G. N., 77
Barnett, Canon S., 12
Barrie, J. M., 60
Bartholomew, H. G., 134
Battenberg, Prince Louis of, 79
Beardsley, Aubrey, 36
Beaverbrook, Lord (*formerly* Max
  Aitken), 74, 121, 149, 150, 154
Bechuanaland, 20, 170
Belfast, 53, 92
Belgium, 45–7, 72, 79, 139, 165
Belloc, Hilaire, 60

Printed in Great Britain by
Thomas Nelson and Sons Ltd, Edinburgh